Four Steps to Revival

Four Steps to Revival

Preparing the Body of Christ for the greatest revival of all time

Dalen Garris

FOUR STEPS TO REVIVAL
Copyright ©2017 by Dalen Garris

All rights reserved. No portion of this book may be reproduced, stored in a retrieval system, or transmitted in any form or by any means—electronic, mechanical, photocopy, recording, scanning, or other—except for brief quotations in critical reviews or articles, without the prior written permission of the publisher.

Unless otherwise noted, Scripture quotations are taken from the King James Version.
Scripture quotations marked ESV are taken from THE ENGLISH STANDARD VERSION. © 2001 by Crossway Bibles, a division of Good News Publishers.

Library of Congress Cataloging-in-Publication Data

ISBN: 0999469401
ISBN 13: 9780999469408

Printed in the United States of America

16 17 18 19 20 [Printer Code] 6 5 4 3 2 1

Dedication

This book is dedicated to all the old Holy Ghost warriors who came out of the Azusa Street revivals and saw in the young hippies of the Jesus Movement a spark of the same fire they had seen 50 years before. They inspired us to believe in this last, great revival promised in the Book of Joel. My prayer and my hope is that this book can help pass that fire on to this next Gideon Generation and inspire them to bring it on home.

Table of Contents

Dedication		v
Preface		ix
Introduction		xi
1	The Cycle of Apostasy and Revival	1
2	Soul Winning, the Secret to Revival	5
3	Six Principles of Revival	29
4	Step 1 Recognition	35
5	Step 2 Repentance	59
6	Step 3 How to Build a Fire in the Church	69
7	Step 4 The Call to Battle	76
8	The Greatest Revival of All Time	82
9	Practical Steps	87
Conclusion		99
About the Author		101

Preface

I GREW UP as a "stone-cold atheist" in the rebellious sixties. I found it impossible to believe in a god that I could not see, feel, or touch. I especially despised Christianity, believing that it was the worst thing that had ever happened to the world. In 1969, however, God gave me a supernatural revelation that He, in fact, existed and that He inhabited the entire universe. Faced with this incredible revelation, I gave up a full scholarship at Boston University to hitchhike around the country to find this God that had revealed Himself to me.

In February 1970, I was saved at a little hippie church in Hollywood, California, right at the beginning of the Jesus Movement. We had very little in resources — just a tiny church with a bunch of young kids that were on fire — but the Spirit and power of God poured out on that church every day. It was like nothing I had ever seen before or since. That changed me and set the course for the rest of my life.

After several exciting years of street ministry across several cities in America, I came to Dallas, Texas, and established a radio broadcast that grew from a fifteen-minute spot in a local market to a thirty-minute broadcast that spread internationally to several countries, from Jerusalem to Asia. My broadcast in Jerusalem was rebroadcast as the *Voice of Jerusalem* on Sky Angel satellite radio across North America for years.

A weekly column that was printed in several newspapers quickly followed the radio broadcast, and that led to a blog and an email list that reached hundreds of subscribers. That exposure led to invitations abroad.

In 2004 I accepted an invitation to come to Kenya to preach on the topic of revival. That led to more trips across sub-Saharan Africa. After twelve years, I have made over forty trips to a dozen countries, preached in over five hundred churches, and seen tens of thousands of souls saved. Hundreds of miracles followed the revivals that were ignited, and fires were generated in hundreds of churches that are still burning today.

During the course of those twelve years in revival, I was asked to put the message down in writing so the members of the churches that had heard the messages would still have them after I had left. The messages that developed and grew over those years have resulted in this book, *Four Steps to Revival*. Over fifty thousand copies have been printed and given away across Africa.

The one enduring great hope I have had all these years is that revival would come to America. I don't believe it will start here because we are not hungry enough to pay the price that true revival requires. But if a revival fire would break out in Africa, I believe it could spread here to America.

America and England evangelized the world. They brought this very same gospel they are now bored with to the entire world, including Africa. Especially Africa! And it is Africa, where people are so hungry that they will literally walk for 12 to 13 hours just to hear the Word of God preached, I believe will birth this final end-time revival God has promised. And maybe, just maybe, that same fire will spread to us here who sent it over there in the first place.

The Word of God tells us repeatedly that mercy brings mercy. May God remember us in mercy, break up the fallow ground of our hearts, and restore unto us the grandeur of His Presence and send revival.

Introduction

THIS BOOK WAS birthed out of a series of messages I gave to a number of churches over the past decade. I have watched as my message of hope and reconciliation transformed and energized them. Time and time again, the excitement that had been generated caused these churches to double, triple, and quadruple in size, sometimes in just a few months. As the churches grew, they spread, and planted hundreds of new churches across Africa. I believe this is a testament to an unfulfilled hunger for God and for a gospel that has real power.

Because the Holy Spirit anointed these messages so much, I was asked to put them into writing so that after I left a church, they would have the messages in book form to refer to. I have been told repeatedly that the really exciting thing about this book was that finally here is a step-by-step plan that makes sense, is easy to understand, and comes right out of the Bible. It just simply works. It is neither theologically complex nor so warm and fuzzy that it has no distinct substance. It is simple, strong, and real. And it works.

The word *revival* is, in most cases, a misnomer because it suggests bringing a dead body back to life again. But throughout history, the great moves of God have been more of a rebellion against an established religious system that had grown cold and secular. Once a body is dead, resuscitation will not bring it back to life. A new life springing up in a new body is needed, not the resurrection of the old apostate system that has died.

I believe that revival is the best hope for a solution to the deep spiritual problems that face our world today. As do many other Christians who have been watching biblical prophecy unfold in the news, I strongly believe that we are living in the last days. While many believe we have little cause to worry because they expect to be raptured out of the troubles that are coming upon the face of the earth, I believe that the church will not only face them but will go through them until Jesus' second coming occurs.

Shakespeare wrote, "All the world is a stage." That is truer than what he might have suspected. All the politics, business, careers, and hobbies of our lives are merely the things in life that we go through that ultimately determine our eternal destiny. The church is supposed to be the landmark and lighthouse that points the way to heaven to a society that is often forgetful of the dual realities of the natural and the spiritual world we live in.

When the church loses its vibrancy and its light grows dim, however, we find ourselves easily enamored with the other things that make up our lives. Our focus shifts from our eternal destiny to our present world, and the urgency of eternal judgment takes a backseat to the more immediate sensory inputs from the world around us. We soon lose our way, forget that this stage we are on is only a test, and lose our edge on what is really important. Life becomes complicated with thorns and snares that pull us with an ever-increasing compulsion further away from true salvation in Jesus Christ.

The only solution for this is a heaven-sent Holy Ghost revival, the kind that breaks out of the sky, filled with power from the throne of God. True revival is a supernatural move of God that grips the church and spreads across the surrounding community with a penetrating conviction of sin and a palpable presence of His power. You feel it more than know it, but it is more real than anything else you ever experienced. The gap between Earth and eternity collapses and nothing else matters.

Without a bright, shining light to point us in the true direction of life, we can only stumble around in darkness. Only a true Holy Ghost revival can light those fires again and make our lighthouses illuminate the path to salvation. Jesus said that if He were lifted up, He would draw all men to Him. That, more than anything, is what revival is all about.

There is time for one more revival. Jesus Christ is coming back to earth soon, but before He comes, the Bible tells us there will be one more last great revival, the greatest revival of all time. Revival does not come without a price, however, and it is that price that this book is about.

All fires must have a match to start them. My prayer is that this booklet will be a match to help ignite a blaze of revival that will burn around the world.

1
The Cycle of Apostasy and Revival

THE TIMES OF apostasy when the church falls away from a close relationship with God, and the times of revival when we are reunited with Him, are cyclical, going all the way back to the time of Joshua in the Old Testament. Whenever there is a great move of God, the church is energized and becomes a vibrant and an embracive part of the lives of its people. Joy and gladness are signs of these times. Prosperity and life uplift not only the church itself but the entire society surrounding it. These are wonderful times!

Within a short while, however, the brightness begins to fade and the wonderful blessings of an intimate walk in the Spirit begin to be taken for granted and are traded in for a fascination with what the world has to offer instead. Our focus slowly shifts from the eternal to the temporal, from the longings of our souls to the lusts of our flesh, from the promises of the invisible to the immediate gratification of the visible. Salvation and religion begin to yield to a cheap and easy grace, one that is less intrusive of our personal lives and less demanding of holiness.

The broad path seems to make much more sense to us and is much easier to travel down. After all, we wonder, why should we endure suffering when Jesus has already suffered in our place on the cross? Religion becomes established, sophisticated, and entrenched in a society that it no longer feels the compulsion to challenge. The persecution that once lit the fires of revival that forged many of our denominations has now dissipated and is no longer considered necessary. We have arrived and are satisfied.

When there is no price to pay, true Christianity does not seem so precious, and it, as with all things cheap, becomes much easier to discard. As the fires of revival die down to simmering embers, the church still retains its shape and structure, but it loses its heart. Church now becomes more about just attending services on Sunday instead of cultivating a close relationship with Jesus and winning the lost.

Revival is the heartbeat of God, and winning the lost is the heartbeat of revival. Jesus did not die so we could have a nice church and a prosperous life but so we would grow up into Him and be a light to win the lost. When we forget that, we miss the entire meaning of the cross. Our focus then shifts from others to ourselves, and slowly our candle begins to dim as the Spirit of God that once drove our churches begins to fade away.

People are often mistaken about what revival is. Many think that the heart of revival is that wonderful feeling we have as the Spirit of God flows through us or the excitement we feel when we see miracles and supernatural manifestations of the Spirit. The picture that runs through our minds is of great crowds of people with their hands raised, singing and praising God as the Holy Spirit pours out all over them like honey. But that is not the true heart of revival. Revival is about the winning of lost souls. This is the whole purpose and heart of revival.

When we become so enamored with how good the flow of the Holy Spirit feels that we lose our agony for lost souls, we end up turning off the faucet of the Spirit. Before long, we are left with nothing but church and a form of godliness. We rarely notice the decrease until it is down to a trickle as we slowly become used to the institution rather than the inspiration. Our candlestick is slowly removed (Revelation 2:5) and we gradually get used to the darkness until we can no longer see the truth anymore.

At such times, God always sends His prophets to call us to repentance. The job of a prophet is not to be a gypsy tea-leaf reader to tell us about our futures, but to call God's people to repentance. It is a job that no one likes, neither the one called as the prophet nor the ones he is called to prophesy to. The true prophet's message never goes along with the current trend but is designed to cause trouble and discomfort as it roots up the foundation of dead works. As a result, prophets are often either ignored and dismissed or persecuted and killed.

One of the signs of apostasy in the church is the flourishing of prophets of "peace and prosperity". Like weeds, they grow out of barren ground and find root in the worldliness of the church. False prophets do not call us to repentance; they call us to repose. There is never any challenge in their prophecies; they only offer promises of peace and prosperity. They do not point us to the fear of God but rather drench us in a permissive gospel that is overflowing in a false sense of peace and love.

The problem is, their definition of the love of God is little more than a warm, fuzzy feeling, a comfortable "relationship" with a God who is our "Daddy." The Word of God, however, defines the love of God as the keeping of His commandments (John 14:15; 15:10; 1 John 5:2–3), which comes through the fear of the Lord. But like pied pipers, these false prophets play the tune that many itching ears in the church want to hear, and they entice us with visions of sugarplums, instead of the fruits of repentance.

Although prophets are not usually accepted in their time, the seeds they plant will find fertile ground in a new generation. The prophet Joel described these hungry souls as beasts that are groaning for pasture but are not able to find it (Joel 1:18). In their search for the truth, this new generation will embrace the words of those prophets whom their fathers dismissed. Those words will ring true in their souls and begin to grow in their hearts to encourage them to reach up in hope for a fresh, new outpouring of God.

Gideon threshed his wheat in secret by the winepress, the wheat being a symbol of the Bread of Life and the winepress of prayer, and so do these God-seekers. They seek the truth of God outside the established liturgies of a church structure that has grown irrelevant and apostate. Like Gideon, the new generation will sense that the existing religious structure is no longer answering the needs of their hearts and will begin to search for something more than what their fathers were offering them.

And so the cycle goes, over and over again. Is this by design of God, or is it a symptom of the failure of human flesh? I do not have the answer to that, but I do know that just as Jesus was a root out of dry ground (Isaiah 53:2) so do great harvests come after times of spiritual drought.

The church is in just such a time as that right now. We are ready for the rain and a subsequent time of harvest, but this time the outpouring of God's Holy Spirit will eclipse all other revivals. As we come out of the spiritual famine that both the prophets Joel and Amos foretold would come just before the coming of the Lord Jesus Christ, the greatest revival of all time is scheduled to arrive.

2
Soul Winning, the Secret to Revival

THE CURRENT GENERATION seems to be enamored with blessings, miracles, and spiritual anointings but are turned off by holiness, the fear of the Lord, and the sufferings of the cross. Perhaps it has always been this way, but I don't remember hearing of a time when the main goal of so many Christians was to be so immersed in "spiritual blessings." When the desire to be spiritual becomes more important than keeping the commandments of God, we find ourselves falling for the same temptation that Eve did when she reached for that fruit in the garden.

Revival is not about miracles, blessings, beautiful experiences, and good times; it is about winning the lost. Period. All the wonderful blessings of the Spirit—the miracles, healings, outpourings, and anointing—are the *results* of revival, not the reason for it. When we take our eyes off winning souls and begin to lose ourselves in the blessings that accompany it, we wind up turning off the faucet to the Spirit of God. When it is all said and done, we are left with nothing but a church, some traditions, and a bunch of faded memories of what it was like when the Spirit of God used to flow in our now-dead church.

When we turn and realize what the heart of God is really yearning for, and we redirect our focus to winning the lost so we are no longer consumed with ourselves, then the primary goal of our lives now lines up with the two Great Commandments: love God and win souls. Then, and only then, will we begin to see a Holy Ghost revival that will rock the heavens and transform the world.

This is the secret of revival.

Soul winning is the very heart of God. It is His deepest desire. The prophet Malachi tells us that God refers to us as His jewels (Malachi 3:17). We are precious in the sight of the Lord, more than what we will ever fully understand. As the King of glory, Jesus left heaven to go through all the trials, temptations, and sufferings of flesh, only to suffer the torture and shame of the cross. And then, even worse, He had to bear all the sins of the world and have His Father turn away from Him as He cried out, *"Lama sabachthani"* (Mark 15:34). All this so we could be with Him in eternity. As David exclaimed, "What is man that thou art mindful of him?" (Psalm 8:4).

Soul winning was so important to Jesus that, as He was about to ascend up into heaven, He left His disciples with this one last request. He was leaving and would not be back for thousands of years, so this was His final plea. Whenever someone who is close to us is leaving us for the final time asks us for one last final request, it always carries a heavier weight for us. Most of us will do everything we can to fulfill that last request. Jesus left us with the Great Commission: "Go ye into all the world, and preach the gospel to every creature" (Mark 16:15).

Sadly, most of us have not even gone into all our neighborhood, never mind the world. But we've done everything else we think a good Christian should do. Everything, that is, except what He asked us to do. Somehow, we have all heard this scripture and ignored it. These excuses may sound familiar:

> "Perhaps it was spoken just to the disciples who were standing there."
> "There are other jobs we can do besides witnessing to the lost".
> "That is someone else's job. I'm not good at that kind of thing. I'm sure the Lord sees me letting my little light shine over in the corner."

Jesus loved the world so much that He gave His life for them. What more could He have done? And now it is our turn. The Lord specifically told us to go – not sit, not wait, not ponder, and certainly not make excuses.

> Whosoever shall call upon the name of the Lord shall be saved. How then shall they call on him in whom they have not believed? and how shall they believe in him of whom they have not heard? and how shall they hear without a preacher? And how shall they preach, except they be sent? as it is written, How beautiful are the feet of them that preach the gospel of peace, and bring glad tidings of good things! (Romans 10:13-15)

If winning souls is the secret to revival, if He has told us to witness to these souls and that they will not get saved unless we do, and if He has told us He will cut off His Spirit from the church until we do, then what are we waiting for?

Luke tells us that Jesus was having dinner in the house of a chief of the Pharisees. After He admonished them about not inviting the poor, maimed, and blind to their feasts, one of the religious men who was there made the comment, "Blessed is he that shall eat bread in the kingdom of God" (Luke 14:15). That sounds like a typical comment for a Pharisee, or even many denominational churchgoers of today, trying to fit in with the conversation but being oblivious to the fact that they were doing the exact opposite of what Jesus was talking about. They were so blind that they just couldn't get it.

Jesus responded by telling them the parable of the great banquet, in which three men were invited to a great banquet but all gave excuses why they could not come. They were too busy for God. The servant was then sent out into the streets to invite the poor, maimed, and blind—the same ones Jesus just admonished the Pharisees about—and bring them to the great banquet. Still having room, the Lord commanded the servant to go into the streets and "compel them to come in" (Luke 14:23) so His house would be filled. But what happened to the original ones who were invited but were too busy? They didn't even get a taste of the supper.

Who is Jesus talking to in this parable? Certainly not to His servant who is running around trying to get everything set up. The message is to the church. Have we become so busy that we are more interested in our own lives than in helping to fulfill the Great Commission by going out into the world to invite the lost to the banquet of salvation? It is God's desire to fill up the banquet room. And if we won't go, He will find someone else to take our place.

As the church, the Bride of Christ, we should have the same passion and desperation to see souls saved that we see in Rachel's cry, when she realized she was not bearing any children for her husband Jacob. In desperation, she grabbed hold of her husband and cried out, "Give me children, or else I die!" (Genesis 30:1). We also should feel that same shame for not bearing fruit for our husband, Jesus Christ, and let it drive us to our knees in desperation to cry out, "Give me souls, or else I die!"

In the Old Testament, a woman's main purpose was to bear children for her husband. They didn't get married to make the bed, wash his socks, or make breakfast; they got married to raise a family. It was, therefore, a shame for a woman to be barren. Even in today's modern society, to have children is one of the greatest desires for women. Women are made with that innate desire built into them.

Like Rachel, we have to want spiritual children badly enough to die. Badly enough to give our lives so that souls will get saved. That is how Jesus felt. He loved souls so much He gave His life for them. He expects us to do the same.

Winning the lost is more than just God's desire. There is a distinct purpose to His plan. When the church is not winning souls, we are like a barren woman to God. Our purpose in serving the Lord is to bear fruit. If we only get saved for our own selves, then why stay alive? Why not get saved and then keel over dead? Why waste the air? Just go to heaven. You're done. Ah, but we are still here aren't we? So perhaps there is a reason why. Maybe it is because we are supposed to fulfill the mission of the Bride of Christ and bear much fruit.

In the parable of the true vine, Jesus tells us that when we abide in Him, we will bring forth much fruit, but if we do not, we will be broken off and cast into the fire (John 15). This does not paint a pleasant picture. Nevertheless, it is clear what God wants. Jesus said He chose us for one purpose: to bring forth fruit and that "your fruit should remain" (John 15:16). This is not about us. This is about God.

"Herein is my Father glorified, that ye bear much fruit; so shall ye be my disciples" (John 15:8). God is glorified when we win souls! We and all creation were created to glorify God, and this is how He is glorified: winning souls. The purpose of winning souls is not, therefore, just to rescue humanity, but that by so doing we would glorify God not only for His mercy and loving-kindness but also for His righteousness and judgment. This was so important that God made Jesus "to be sin for us, who knew no sin; that we might be made the righteousness of God in him" (2 Corinthians 5:21).

God had a plan, and it was so important to Him that it cost Him everything. He ripped out His heart and allowed it to be crushed, beaten, and killed so we could be delivered from death and spend eternity with Him, so that in the final analysis all the glory would go to God.

What a price to pay, but what a glory it is to inherit!

Bearing Fruit
In writing about Adam and Eve, the apostle Paul tells us, "Notwithstanding she shall be saved in childbearing" (1 Timothy 2:15). Is he saying all women who do not have babies are going to hell? Of course not. He is talking about the church! As Eve was the bride of the first Adam, so the church is the Bride of Christ, the second Adam. And as such, she is commanded to bring forth fruit. Do not mistake this as some light comment that Paul tosses off. This is a serious commandment about the necessity of winning souls.

Jesus is recorded in four places in the Gospels as saying that every tree that does not bring forth good fruit will be cut down and thrown in the fire (Matthew 3:10; 7:19; Luke 3:9; John 15:2) In the parable of the true vine, Jesus said that if we abide in Him, we will bring forth much fruit. If we don't abide in Him, however, we will wither and will be cast forth into the fire (John 15). Yikes! In the fire? Is that a coincidental reference? I doubt it. The principle is clear. Our primary purpose is to win souls. If we do not, then we are a dead branch, lifeless without the sap of the Holy Spirit flowing through us.

It is often said that our purpose in life is to glorify God. Well, this is how we glorify the Father: going out and winning souls: "Herein is my Father glorified, that ye bear much fruit" (John 15:8).

Singing songs and lifting our hands in praises are great, but if souls are dropping off into hell while we are singing our songs, then how does that glorify God?

Jesus went one step deeper: "So shall ye be my disciples."

And what happens if we do not bear much fruit? Ah, do you see my point? Our walk with God, even our very purpose for living is tied irrevocably to winning lost souls. And if we, as dead branches without

Christ in us, are thrown into the fire, where do you think we will spend eternity?

Winning souls for Christ is not just another function of the church; it is a command to the church. God told Adam, Noah, Abraham, and Jacob to multiply and bear fruit. That command is to us also.

I have listened to some pastors say that their church doesn't do evangelism because they believe they have more of a calling to minister to their flock than to go out into the world and invite the lost. Other pastors are not so bold as to say something that ignorant, but their lack of effort to reach out to the unsaved and their absence of outreaches to the lost tell the same tale. Others have intermittent outreaches that will only take them to easy places where there is no resistance or there's not that much sin and crime so as to avoid any problems. They don't mind constructing a building somewhere, painting a church, or doing a puppet show, but to venture out into a community to challenge and invite sinners to come to salvation? No, they actually believe they are not supposed to become that radical; They believe that, instead, they should just win them through more indirect means.

Why are we so afraid to tell people the truth of the gospel? Why do we shrink from telling them of the judgment to come and hope that if we only tell them about love they will repent? Is it because we fear our own judgment? Is our own lack of righteousness and fear of God convicting us and keeping us from standing in holy boldness to declare the truth?

God places the requirement on us as His watchmen to warn sinners of the judgment to come if they do not repent. This is made clear in the passages about the watchman on the wall (Ezekiel 3; 33). The consequences for us are fatal if we do not: "When I say unto the wicked, Thou shalt surely die; and thou givest him not warning, nor speakest to warn the wicked from his wicked way, to save his life; the same wicked man shall die in his iniquity; but his blood will I require at thine hand" (Ezekiel 3:18).

Chilling words. And yet, isn't the act of going out to rescue sinners from an eternity in hell a demonstration of the love of God through us? Wouldn't you want someone to warn you if you were headed for hell? Jesus said, "Whatsoever ye would that men should do to you, do ye even so to them: for this is the law and the prophets" (Matthew 7:12). The whole law and the prophets are summed up in this statement! The entire Word of God is focused on winning the lost, and God commands us to be the instrument He uses to shower them with His mercy.

The Great Commandments
All the law and the prophets hang on the two Great Commandments:

> Master, which is the great commandment in the law? Jesus said unto him, Thou shalt love the Lord thy God with all thy heart, and with all thy soul, and with all thy mind. This is the first and great commandment. And the second is like unto it, Thou shalt love thy neighbour as thyself. On these two commandments hang all the law and the prophets. (Matthew 22:36–40)

Everything that determines our eternal destination and our everlasting relationship with Almighty God can be distilled down to these two commandments: love God with all your heart, soul, body, and strength, and love your neighbor as yourself. If you do not fulfill those two, it won't matter how many of the others you do.

Turning our focus around from ourselves to others is pivotal in our entire Christian walk. This is a principle of revival: the gospel is not about us; it is about others. How many times are we admonished throughout the New Testament to love our brothers? Can you see that our attitude toward God is reflected in our attitude toward others?

I believe the reverse is true also. If we really love God with all our heart, we will go after the lost, because we know that helping to deliver the lost out of the kingdom of darkness is so precious to God that He gave His Son so they could be saved. He tells us to do the same. This is not a request but a command straight from the mouth of God: Go into all the world, preach the gospel, and make disciples.

The Church at Ephesus
The church today will participate in all kinds of projects, charities, programs, you name it, but she shrinks from the battle because she has lost her fear of God, her zeal for what God called her for, and her sense of victory over sin and death.

Are you too busy with "church stuff" to be an active soul winner? Do you think that being busy with all the programs and events your church engages in will be a good enough substitute for being a witness? That is a common belief in the church world. We are busy, busy, busy with church activities because it is so much easier to follow a prepackaged program than Jesus' command to go to the streets. But substituting carnal works for God's original command will never satisfy God. It is the same mistake Cain made when he offered vegetables instead of blood at the altar of God.

I'm sure Cain worked very hard. He might have even been bitter that Able didn't do much besides hang around watching the sheep all day while he labored all day in his fields to produce some very good vegetables. But it wasn't what God required. The price of sin is blood, and all the good works (or vegetables) in the world cannot satisfy the requirements for atonement. And neither will organized efforts, projects, and comprehensive programs, books, videos, and other carnal efforts ever be a substitute for the simple things that God requires: read, pray, and witness.

The church at Ephesus also thought they could substitute good works for going out to win the lost. In Revelation 2, Jesus calls out to them saying that He knows their works, their labor and patience, and even how they hate sin. Oh, they are rich in all kinds of "church stuff," but they have lost their first love.

That first love is what you felt when you first got saved. Do you remember how you felt when that burden of sin was first lifted off you? When you felt free for the first time in your life? When you felt you had passed from death into life? You were so excited that you wanted to tell everyone what Jesus Christ had done for you.

But most believers have lost that fresh excitement and have settled into "church as usual." The vibrancy and excitement they felt as babes in Christ has dulled over time and are no longer burning with that same holy fire. We have left our first love.

So what does God say to us who are like that? Repent and do those first works, or else He will come quickly—no fooling around—and will remove our candlestick. Without the candlestick, we have no light but are in darkness, stumbling around lost.

Doing church stuff like attending services, singing songs, giving canned goods to the poor and toys to needy children at Christmas, are great things to do, but it will not stave off the judgment of God.

Charity
In 1 Corinthians 13, Paul explained the utter bedrock importance of charity over carnal works. You can do all the religious stuff—speak with tongues, prophesy, understand mysteries, and have the faith to move mountains—but if you don't have charity, it will profit you nothing. What good would it be to be the greatest big shot in the world for God if you don't care about the lost? The whole purpose of what you were called for is wrapped up in the call to bear much fruit. God doesn't need prima donnas; He needs servants.

And what about the good works we do? If you give all your goods to the poor—*all* of them—what good is it if you have not told them the gospel so that they can spend eternity in heaven? If you allow your body to be burned so that you give the ultimate sacrifice, what will that accomplish in helping to save a sinner from hell? This is not about works for works' sake. You will never impress God with your efforts, intelligence, or theological credentials, or with the amount of your sacrifice if those things are not done to win souls.

Charity is the giving of yourself out of love so souls can be saved. Fulfill that and you will fulfill the two Great Commandments and, by default, the law and the prophets.

God's Promise of Blessing

Would you like to know how to curry favor with God so He will not only answer your prayers but also pour out blessings on you that you cannot contain? The answer is to have mercy on the lost. This is very important to God.

Isaiah 58 starts out by echoing a cry that the church that is not in revival is all too familiar with: why doesn't God answer our prayers? We have fasted and prayed; we have kept the commandments; we take delight in approaching God; but nothing happens. Why, God? What's wrong?

I was holding revival services in Nigeria several years ago when a minister asked me to come to a pastors' conference he was holding in the city of Abuja. He said they had tried everything they could think of to bring a move of the Holy Ghost, but there was still no revival. "Something is wrong," he said, "and we need to know what it is." It wasn't a matter of what they were doing; it was what they were *not* doing.

We fast and pray, but what is it that we are praying for? Are we afflicting our souls for others, or for our own things? What is our focus, ourselves or others?

Let's take a look at what the prophet Isaiah said:

> Is not this the fast that I have chosen? to loose the bands of wickedness, to undo the heavy burdens, and to let the oppressed go free, and that ye break every yoke? (Isaiah 58:6)

Is the intent of your fasting and prayer to break those shackles of bondage that sinners are under, to free them from that heavy burden of sin that is weighing them down and set them free? People don't choose to go to hell. They are enticed by their own lusts and the desires of their flesh and dragged into captivity. Once they are brought into bondage, they need someone to help them escape. Isaiah goes on to say this:

> Is it not to deal thy bread to the hungry, and that thou bring the poor that are cast out to thy house? When thou seest the naked, that thou cover him; and that thou hide not thyself from thine own flesh? (Isaiah 58:7)

What kind of bread is the prophet talking about here? The Bread of Life. What kind of house are we supposed to be bringing the poor into? The house of God. What kind of clothing should we be covering them with? The robes of righteousness. Are we in pursuit of the hungry, poor, and naked in Spirit to help bring them into a walk with God and provide the spiritual sustenance they need?

God promises us that if we will turn our attention to these acts of mercy, our light will then break forth as the morning, like the sunshine after a long dark night:

> Then shall thy light break forth as the morning. (Isaiah 58:8)

Are you going through difficult times and left wondering why you are going through such difficult circumstances? How would you like to see the light break forth and spill out into your daily life? Perhaps God is waiting on you to sow mercy on others so He can sow mercy upon you.

Isaiah went on to point out in verse 8 that if we are focused on the well-being of others, then our health will spring forth speedily. Could it be that many of us suffer needlessly simply because we don't have mercy on the lost? Scripture tells us that we reap what we sow. If we will not bring health to those around us, do you really expect Him to bring health to you? This may seem a bit harsh to some people, but I know that God uses trouble like a fine tool to take the trouble out of our lives. But if we do these things, the Lord says that the glory of the Lord will be our protection and will surround us:

> Your righteousness shall go before you; the glory of the
> Lord shall be your rear guard. (Isaiah 58:8, esv)

When you walk into a store, do people sense there is just something different about you? Can they feel the heat from the glow of God's glory around you? Can they smell the incense of His anointing on you? Do you want to walk in His presence like that? If you do, then turn your attention to those around you who are on their way to hell and need someone to help them, and minister to them so that God can, in turn, bless you.

> Then shalt thou call, and the Lord shall answer; thou shalt
> cry, and he shall say, Here I am. (Isaiah 58:9)

A friend of mine once said that true honor is not when you have a great position or title but when God hears your prayers and answers them. Oh, to be able to cry out to God and know He not only will hear the cry of His servant but will call back to you, "Here I am," as He answers your call! Can there be any honor greater than that?

> If thou draw out thy soul to the hungry, and satisfy the
> afflicted soul; then shall thy light rise in obscurity, and thy
> darkness be as the noon day: and the Lord shall guide thee
> continually, and satisfy thy soul in drought, and make fat
> thy bones: and thou shalt be like a watered garden, and like
> a spring of water, whose waters fail not. (Isaiah 58:10–11)

"Feed my sheep," Jesus told Peter. "If you love me, feed my sheep." The simple call of the Great Shepherd to us is to show others the same mercy He has had on us. If we will, God promises us these incredible blessings and to lead us in His Spirit and watch over us. He will raise you up as a light in the darkness so others will be able to see His glory in you. He will not leave you in the obscurity of some dark corner where you are an unused unknown. As a good businessman who values all his assets and uses them to gain a profit, He will be able to use you in ways you never expected because you sowed mercy. When all others suffer spiritual drought and famine, God will remember His covenant with us because we had mercy on others.

It is in the dynamics of sowing mercy that we untie the hands of God in our life. He cannot go against His own word. We reap what we sow. When we sow mercy, we open the door for Him to use us. If we are not merciful to others, then our Christian life stagnates because there is no driving power of God in it. The blessings that are driven by the promises of God can work only when we fulfill the conditions in His Word. If you want God to bless your ministry and use you in supernatural ways, sow mercy and your light will rise in obscurity.

Let me end this with one more promise from God's Word:

> They that shall be of thee shall build the old waste places: thou shalt raise up the foundations of many generations; and thou shalt be called, The repairer of the breach, The restorer of paths to dwell in. (Isaiah 58:12)

Here is a final promise in this chapter that gives us the secret to revival. If we will answer the call to go forth shining His light into the darkness, we will build the foundations of the church that has been broken down from years of apostasy and neglect. We will be like Nehemiah, who rebuilt the wall of safety around the Temple and restored the paths to revival. We will reclaim the glory of God in the church.

What a calling! What a legacy! In eternity, others will come up to us and say, "Oh, we know who you are. You're the ones who repaired the breach and brought in the great revival in the last days."

This is the promise of God. His promises are sure. If you will yield to His call, He will fulfill His word to you. His conditions are simple: do unto others as you would have them do unto you. Sow mercy, breathe charity, pour out your life to others. Pick up the cross and follow Him, and He will lead you into His glory.

I sincerely believe that if we refuse to have mercy on the lost we will stand before God in judgment and have to give an account for why we refused to obey this command. After all that has been written in His Word, to refuse this one command will be looked upon as sheer rebellion. As James said, "Therefore to him that knoweth to do good, and doeth it not, to him it is sin" (James 4:17). You can't say you didn't know. The Bible is saturated with admonishments to witness to the lost and make disciples.

Wise Solomon wrote,

> "If thou forbear to deliver them that are drawn unto death, and those that are ready to be slain; If thou sayest, Behold, we knew it not; doth not he that pondereth the heart consider it? and he that keepeth thy soul, doth not he know it? and shall not he render to every man according to his works?" (Proverbs 24:11–12).

At issue here is the subject of mercy. We all need it – and we will especially need it in the Day of Judgment – but mercy does not come free. Many church people feel, for some reason, that just because they go to church they will be deserving of the mercy of God, but that is not the case. You have to sow mercy to get mercy. And according to James 2:13, if you have shown no mercy, there will be none for you on the Day of Judgment.

My pastor used to tell us that if you don't plant the seeds of mercy in your garden, there will be no fruit there to eat when you need it. The proverb tells us, "Whoso stoppeth his ears at the cry of the poor, he also shall cry himself, but shall not be heard" (Proverbs 21:13). Imagine, if you will, that all the things in life you rely upon for your security are suddenly taken away and you are left in dire straits. You're expecting God to deliver you, but when you cry, there is no answer. Instead, you get that dead silence that comes back from a shut door. You call out for mercy, but there is none because you didn't sow mercy on the poor, the fatherless, or the lost. You just lived for yourself. And now, when you need that mercy, there is nothing on the tree.

Think that's severe? Consider what God said in Proverbs 1:24–32 to those who refused to listen when He called and ignored all God's reproof: He will laugh and mock at them when their time of fear and desolation comes.

If we do not hearken to the call from God to go out and sow mercy, we also will call, but we will get the same response that we gave Him.

The Judgment of the Sheep and the Goats
One of the most damning passages related to this subject that confronts us is Jesus' parable about the judgment of the sheep and the goats (Matthew 25:31–46). He said the Lord will divide them into heaven and hell, not on the basis of personal works or on religious accomplishments or even on individual righteousness, but on whether or not they had mercy on the lost and needy.

He will turn first to the sheep and usher them into heaven. Why? Because when He was hungry, thirsty, naked, sick, in prison, or a stranger, they took care of Him. Then He will turn to the goats and condemn them to hell because they did not minister to Him.

What made the difference between the sheep and the goats, and how does that apply to you? When you saw them in the prison of sin, did you visit them by witnessing to them? When you saw those who were hungry for truth, did you feed them with the Bread of Life? When you saw they were thirsty, did you give them the Living Waters? Did you clothe them with the robes of righteousness? Did you even invite them to come to church? Or did you sit in your church and hope that somehow they would wander in to get saved? Didn't you realize that your lifelessness and lack of true charity would be the very thing that turned them away?

The goats will answer back, "When did we see you hungry or thirsty or in prison?" But the answer from Jesus comes, "Inasmuch as ye did it not to one of the least of these, ye did it not to me" (Matthew 25:45).

Chilling words. Did you not see them out there all around you on the roads of life? Or did you think that your only responsibility was to minister unto the Lord? Unfortunately, most Sunday services are filled with would-be Christians who think that by showing up at the church they are somehow serving God. There is no conviction or compulsion to take the message of the gospel any further than the front door of their church. These are the goats.

Jesus' final comment to them is this: "These shall go away into everlasting punishment: but the righteous into life eternal" (Matthew 25:46).

The Lord considers our lack of mercy on lost souls wicked, but He also considers our mercy on others to be righteous.

How can we expect God to send revival until we have repented of our lack of compassion, refusing to give sinners the words of life that were given to us? Mercy drives revival. Without it, we not only cut ourselves off from a move of God, but we also place ourselves in jeopardy of damnation.

Again, the Word of God tells us what we must do:

> With the merciful thou wilt shew thyself merciful. (2 Samuel 22:26)

> Charity shall cover the multitude of sins. (1 Peter 4:8)

> He shall have judgment without mercy, that hath shewed no mercy; and mercy rejoiceth against judgment. (James 2:13)

> Therefore to him that knoweth to do good, and doeth it not, to him it is sin. (James 4:17)

And some may ask, "When did we see You, Lord, when You were in this distress?" And He will say:

> Inasmuch as ye did it not to one of the least of these, ye did it not to me. (Matthew 25:45)

That should be enough to sit us back down and reevaluate our Christian walk. Have we walked past the sick and dying and justified our indifference? What excuse did we use to ignore the specter of hell in those we saw around us every day?

The Parable of the Talents

Two of the parables Jesus shared with His disciples—the parable of the talents (Matthew 25) and the parable of the pounds (Luke 19)—tell basically the same lesson. That lesson is that God gives us all certain things of value that we are supposed to take out into the world and use to promote the kingdom of God. Two servants in both parables did not. One hid his single talent in the ground; the other hid his pound in a napkin.

They both knew that God was a "hard man." Well then why didn't they do something with what God had given them? They knew what He expected of them. This was not a case of ignorance or stupidity. They just refused. They didn't even give it to the banker so the Lord could get interest on it. In other words, they didn't even tithe so at least someone else could use it!

And what did God do to them because of their sin? In one parable, He called the servant "wicked" and in the other He threw the servant into "outer darkness." This is not a picture of heaven. This is the place reserved for sinners.

Is it any different in the parable of the wedding feast (Luke 14)? Everybody made excuses of why they couldn't serve the Lord, and as a result, the Lord was angry. His command is still valid today:

> Go out quickly into the streets and lanes of the city, and bring in hither the poor, and the maimed, and the halt, and the blind.... And compel them to come in, that my house may be filled. (Luke 14:21, 23)

What will happen to the guys who made excuses? None of those who were invited, not even one of them, will taste of His supper. Why? Because they were focused on themselves instead of serving the Lord, and they missed the marriage supper of the Lamb.

The Parable of the Good Samaritan
In Luke, a lawyer, seeking to justify himself, asked Jesus the most important question in life: "What shall I do to inherit eternal life?" (Luke 10:25). This is the number one question of all time. How do I escape the pits of hell? This guy thought he could trap Jesus with some complicated set of rules and bylaws that would circumvent the simplicity of His message. But Jesus answered him with the parable of the Good Samaritan (Luke 10:30–37):

It begins with a man who is traveling from Jerusalem to Jericho. Jerusalem, the city of God, is the highest city in Israel, while Jericho, the city of sin, is the lowest city, near the Dead Sea, and is the city that Joshua cursed. This man was on the road of life, backsliding into sin. Along the way, the devil attacked him and left him dying in his sins by the side of the road. He was bleeding to death in the dirt, dying in his sin.

Along came a priest—a man of the clergy, a pastor, bishop, or some other type of ecclesiastical minister—supposedly a man of God who we would expect to be the first to extend a hand of mercy to those who are lost and dying in sin. But what did the priest do? He scooted himself over to the other side of the road and completely avoided the dying man! "Oh no, this sinner should have come to church where he could have listened to me preach, and then he would have gotten saved. But he didn't come, and now he is dying in his sins. Well, that is the choice he has made and now he will have to suffer the consequences." And so the pastor passed on and he left him in the dirt!

Next came a Levite. Levites were the ministers of the tabernacle just like we are ministers of the church. So he was just like a regular church-going Christian today. Surely, he would help this man out. He was on his way to church, clean and dressed in his staunchly pressed Sunday clothes. But if he stooped to pick up this sinner, his nice, new clothes would get all dirty and bloody, and then he would be too dirty to go to services. What did this upright, staunch church person do? He did the same as the priest! He left him in the dirt to die. Most likely, the Levite figured that this sinner was just a drunkard, a prostitute, or some other type of filthy sinner, and probably would never get saved anyway.

How many of us have not done the same thing as we head off in our Sunday best on our way to church, thinking that we are doing our duty by being religious, all the while ignoring the call of Jesus' Great Commission to save the lost while they are dying in sin all around us?

But then a Samaritan came along. Samaritans were considered the lowest members of Jewish society. This Samaritan not only stops but also poured out wine and oil to heal the man's wounds. Here wine represents the Spirit of God and oil represents the anointing of the Holy Spirit. This man prayed for this sinner right there in the dirt where he was! Then he picked him up and brought him to an inn (the church) where he adjured the innkeeper to make sure this man was taken care of until he returned.

Now then, what was the original question? Was it about being a good Christian or doing good works? No! The question was, how do I escape the pits of hell? How do I escape judgment? Your eternal destiny does not depend on your position in the church or how clean you appear in your Christian walk. This is about having mercy on the lost and dying. That's the answer Jesus gave, and He is the one whom you will be standing in front of.

You can choose what you would like, but as for me, I don't want to end up in the same place as the priest and the Levite. They chose to ignore the lost and dying as they traveled down their road of life, all the while thinking their religiousness would be sufficient to save them. The Word of God gives us a stiff warning about ignoring the lost.

> If thou forbear to deliver them that are drawn unto death, and those that are ready to be slain; if thou sayest, Behold, we knew it not; doth not he that pondereth the heart consider it? And he that keepeth thy soul, doth not he know it? And shall not he render to every man according to his works? (Proverbs 24:11-12)

Blind Bartimaeus

I use many passages when preaching to a church about revival, but I always like to end with one message: the story of blind Bartimaeus (Mark 10:46–52).

In the story Jesus was passing through the city of Jericho on His way to Jerusalem, on His way to die at Calvary. As He passed by, nearly the whole town came out to meet Him. This was at the end of His ministry, so everyone knew who He was and had heard of all the wonderful things He had done. Everybody was there: the mayor, the politicians, the bishops and pastors, all the church people. Everyone wanted to get a glimpse at this Man who many believed was the Messiah.

Along the way, a blind beggar was sitting on the side of the road. Because he was blind, he was rejected by society and considered unclean. No one wanted to even touch him lest they also become unclean. There was no welfare to take care of him, and even his family has rejected him. He was simply left to sit on the side of the road in the dirt, with all the filth dropping on him from the animals that passed by. Starving, he begged for just a crust of bread to make it through the day. But that's not the worst part. The worst part was, he had no hope. Tomorrow would be the same as today, or even worse. He would always be blind, rejected, starving, and begging.

But then he heard that Jesus was passing this way! This was the Man who had healed blind eyes. He had cleansed the lepers, raised the dead, and spoken with the authority of the power of God! This was his one chance, the chance of a lifetime! And He was passing right before him. He had to get hold of Jesus!

So he started crying out, "Jesus, thou son of David, have mercy on me" (verse 47).

But what did the church people do? They told him to shut up. "You're bothering the Master. You are just some filthy, cursed beggar! How dare you lift your voice!"

But Bartimaeus shouted all the louder, "Thou son of David, have mercy on me" (verse 48).

And Jesus stopped. He commanded His disciples to bring Bartimaeus to Him and asked him, "What wilt thou that I should do unto thee?" (verse 51).

Bartimaeus responded, "Lord, that I might receive my sight" (verse 51). He was living in darkness and couldn't see. He desperately needed the light of Jesus Christ, needed to be saved and delivered from the death of sin. He needed Jesus to save his soul!

One time when I read this account, the Lord revealed to me that because there were so many people surrounding Him, it would not have been possible for Jesus to have actually heard Bartimaeus with His physical ears over all the other noise. It wasn't his voice that Jesus heard. He heard the cry of the blind man's heart. That is what stopped Jesus in His tracks. He heard his heart crying out to Him.

Friend, can you hear the cry of the blind man's heart? The sound isn't coming from inside your church. It is coming from out there on the streets from the poor, the blind, the sick, and the lame—from those who are not coming to your church. Are we like the people who surround Jesus with their religious postures but tell the spiritually sick and lame to be quiet? Or can we hear the cry of their hearts?

Dear God, forgive us. Forgive us for "having church". We have forgotten what we were saved for. Are we so full of ourselves that we can no longer hear the cry of the lost?

One Last Story
Allow me to tell one last story in this chapter that illustrates this principle. A few years ago, I was at a revival prayer meeting one evening (at least that was what they called it), and I noticed that the people there were praying for their churches, their pastors, the sick, the music—everything and everybody, except for lost souls! I wondered why they weren't praying for the very thing that revival was all about?

As I was sitting there, the Lord showed me a vision: I saw a large wharf jutting into the ocean. It was three times the width of a normal pier and was full of people. It was a beautiful sunny day, and the people on the wharf were dressed in beautiful clothes with vibrant colors. Everyone seemed so happy, and I could see the joy of the Lord on their faces. These people were really saved and praising Jesus. Everyone was going around blessing each other. Many were laying hands on people and prophesying over them about all kinds of wonderful things. What a beautiful sight!

And then my vision expanded out to the ocean around them. In great contrast to the bright colors I saw on the wharf, the ocean looked dark and cold in a gunmetal gray color, almost as if it were in black and white. The waters were rough and choppy with waves breaking everywhere. Out in the waters I saw hundreds of people drowning, waving their arms and crying out for help as the waves were crashing over them. I tried calling to the people on the dock for them to go help these drowning people, to throw some life preservers out to them. Or better yet, to jump into the water and pull them to safety. But no one could hear me. They just kept on blessing each other, smiling and having a wonderful time.

And then I realized, it wasn't that the people on the wharf didn't care about those who were drowning all around them. Oh, they cared, alright. They just couldn't <u>hear</u> them. They were so full of church that they could not hear the cries of the lost.

"Whoso stoppeth his ears at the cry of the poor, he also shall cry himself, but shall not be heard" (Proverbs 21:13).

3
Six Principles of Revival

AS A FOUNDATION to discussing the steps that the church needs to follow to help facilitate an outpouring of God's Spirit, I'd like to discuss six principles that are vital to understand if we ever expect God to move in revival. I have seen these same principles at work in every revival throughout history that I have studied. They have to do with the believers' attitude and the intents of our hearts and must be in place before any revival will break forth. Without these principles guiding our attitude, nothing we do will work.

1. Revival Is About Winning the Lost

The first principle of revival is to understand that revival is not about how good you feel, how exciting your services are, or how many wonderful blessings you have received. Revival is about winning the lost – first, foremost, and always. The primary reason God sends revival is so that the church will rise up and shine the light of salvation to the millions of lost souls who are on their way to hell.

In order for the church to shine that light effectively, the message of the gospel must be delivered with power, real power, from God. If there is no power in our message, then there is nothing to distinguish the church from the world. If we are no different than the world, then our salt has lost its savor and lost souls will look elsewhere for something to satisfy the longing in the depths of their souls that only God can fulfill. In writing to the Corinthians, Paul boldly proclaimed that he did not come with words of man's wisdom but in the demonstration of the Spirit and power of God so that your faith would not rest in the wisdom of men but in the power of God (1 Corinthians 2:1–5)

Again and again throughout the New Testament, we are told about the power of God to salvation. Without that power, our gospel message is nothing more than just another philosophy about life, someone's ideas about God, and possesses nothing more than a "form of godliness but denying the power thereof." And the admonition from Paul follows: "From such turn away" (2 Timothy 3:5). The reason God sends revival is so the church will burn with a holy fire and exhibit the illuminating and liberating power of God unto salvation. When that fire is burning, souls will come and know the difference between what the gospel has to offer and what the world offers, and they can plant their hope in something real and tangible—the substance of things hoped for.

2. The Gospel Is Not About You

The second principle the church needs to grasp in order to experience revival is that the gospel of Jesus Christ is not about you; it is about others. Most of the messages I hear from pulpits, books, and televangelists today, however, focus on what God can do for *you*, how God wants to bless and prosper *you*, and how the promises are yours for the taking.

While I am all for being blessed by God, it is not the primary reason Jesus died on the cross, neither is it the crucified path of the sufferings of the body of Christ that we are called to walk. He calls for us to deny ourselves if we are to come after him:

> If any man will come after me let him deny himself, and take up his cross daily, and follow me. For whosoever will

> save his life shall lose it: but whosoever will lose his life for
> my sake, the same shall save it. (Luke 9:23)

Jesus didn't die to make us rich. Jesus died to save sinners from hell, and He calls us to follow Him into that same calling in fulfilling the Great Commission by preaching the gospel and making disciples. This is the message of Calvary. If you are not able to grasp this concept, you will never understand the cross.

Until believers get their focus off themselves, God cannot begin to bring revival. He needs shepherds who will give their lives for the sheep before He brings in all those precious souls to them.

3. Everything in God Has a Price

The third principle to understand is that nothing in God is free. Everything has a price. And the price for revival is high, so high, in fact, that I believe this is the reason why true Holy Ghost revivals are so rare. Few people are willing to pay that high a price, especially for people they don't even know. God has to give you a deep burden for the lost to birth the kind of dedication that drives a person to the level of fasting, prayer, and sacrifice that is called for in any revival.

True spiritual labor involves more than just putting your time in, as if working at a regular job. It calls for a brokenness deep in your soul that drives your passion to a burning intensity that will scale any wall and tear down any obstacle that stands in the way of your prayers reaching up to the throne of God and fulfilling your mission. This is not a casual encounter with God but a determined battle against the flesh and anything carnal that stands in the way. You have to want revival with all your heart to pay this kind of price.

The wonderful thing is, if you ask God to give you this burden, He will. But it is up to you to go get it from Him. It's not free. You cannot expect to sit in church and wait for God to drop a revival into your waiting lap; it will not happen. At some point, you will have to get up and *do* something. As the old saying goes, if you keep on doing the things you have been doing, then you will always have the things you have. If you want something different, you are going to have to do something different. If you do nothing, nothing will happen. Faith without works is dead. There is a price to pay.

4. No Revival Comes Without Repentance
The fourth principle of revival is that no revival comes without repentance, both corporately and personally. I will cover this in depth later in chapter 5, but suffice it to say, if our churches were in the place they should be, they would already have the Spirit of God pouring out and wouldn't need to be revived. Repentance changes us. Some may argue that there are times when the church is more subdued and is not necessarily in need of repentance, but I would disagree. When the Spirit of the Lord is moving, there is excitement, and souls get saved. But God is holy and will not move through a dirty vessel, whether that is a church or a person. The only way to clean the vessel so that God can move in it is through repentance.

Whatever has been blocking revival in a person or a church has to be purged. The same rules regarding leprosy in a physical house (Leviticus 14) apply to spiritual leprosy in the house of God. If leprosy was found in a house, everything had to be pulled out, the walls scraped and cleansed, and the house be allowed to heal. If after that cleansing the leprosy continued to spread, then the entire house had to be torn down and dumped outside the camp. Repentance cleanses the church in the same way. If we repent, God can move among us. If we do not, or if our repentance is not complete, the church and all that is in it still has that spiritual leprosy and is destined to be dumped outside the spiritual camp.

5. Revivals Must Be Prayed In
There is no other way to birth a move of God. Prayer moves God. If you want God to send revival, you have to pray it in. It's that simple. All the other things that you may do in your Christian life affect you

or those around you, but prayer moves God. Look throughout history and you will find that before any significant move of God has happened, you will find a group of determined people in deep, contending prayer. Often it is only a few people, but it is always with a contending tenacity that refuses to take no for an answer.

I once asked a friend why it was so hard for us to read and pray. He replied, "That's easy. It's because it's so important." So it is. Reading the Bible along with fasting and prayer are the active tools we are given to facilitate the works of God and the weapons we are given to fight the powers of darkness. No wonder Satan attacks these three things harder than anything else in our Christian life. He knows the power we have in them and can only hope to discourage us from learning how powerful they really are. With reading, prayer, and fasting, we can literally change the world.

Satan's primary attack is to keep believers from reading and prayer, but he especially wants to keep us from attaining a level of intensity in it. If he can keep us satisfied with crumbs, we will never feast on the banquet. Anemic prayer or conversational prayer does not move mountains. Neither does it break through any barriers to reach the throne of God. Yes, it is true that God can hear even the faintest cry of the heart, but many use that reasoning to succumb to a quiet time that cannot be heard past the ceiling because there is no passion in their prayers. It is not about the decibels that you reach in prayer; it is about the depth of passion and desperation. James, using Elijah as an example about the effectiveness of passion in prayer, wrote, "The effectual fervent prayer of a righteous man availeth much" (James 5:16). In other words, if you want it to rain, you have to pray like Elijah.

The depth and intensity of prayer that is required to pray in revivals are higher than most casual Christians are willing to pray for any length of time. History shows, however, that God sometimes requires years of deep passionate pleading for revival from His saints before He begins to shake the earth. But when the hearts of desperate believers are fixed and determined to accept nothing but victory, their prayers will move God. Nothing else will do.

6. Someone Must Be a Vision Bearer

The sixth and final principle of revival is that someone has to have a vision in order to lead the church into revival. Someone has to be able to see past the horizon of time and situation, past circumstances and present realities, and see what God has in store for those who have the faith to receive it. Before any revival breaks out, a man or woman of God with a burning vision is needed to blaze the trail and lead the people of God to revival. He or she sees it before it comes, and they foster that same vision, faith, and enduring desire in those around them to pick up the torch and spread the fire.

These are the vision-bearers for their generation. They are never the normal type of person but are always different, separate, and intense. They breathe a different air, see a different light, embrace the impossible, and have the courage to believe God. They are the ones who hold up the torch that lights the fire of revival for everyone else to follow.

Someone has to start the process, and these vision-bearers are the ones who answer the call.

4
Step 1 Recognition

THE FIRST STEP to seeing revival come is to first recognize that no matter how good we think our church is, we need to acknowledge that we are not in revival right now. We have to realize we are no longer in the place of blessing where we may have been once. Our walls are broken down, the temple is destroyed, and our churches have been carried away to a Babylon where we are still trying to hold on to our religious conventions in a vain attempt to convince ourselves we are still right with God.

The kingdom of Babylon that had captured and destroyed Jerusalem was a place of spiritual death for the church and for Israel. Because the Israelites had forsaken the laws of God for so many generations, God banished them from Jerusalem, the Holy City. He allowed the Babylonian army to come, break down the walls protecting the Israelites, and then carry them away to Babylon for seventy years. The story of their return to Jerusalem is the greatest story of revival in the Bible. When we do the same things that the Israelites did, we will get the same results, both to the banishment of a spiritual Babylon and also to the restoration of the church through revival.

In chapter 2 of the book of Nehemiah, as Nehemiah viewed the rubble of his once-proud city in the cool stillness of the night, he must have felt the desolation that had lain there for almost seventy years. The destruction of Jerusalem was an enormous display of the judgments of God on His own people because they had refused to hearken to Him. Before we can ever begin the task of rebuilding the walls of the city of God, we have to first acknowledge the sins of our people and view the rubble as Nehemiah did:

> I went out by night by the gate of the valley, even before the dragon well, and to the dung port, and viewed the walls of Jerusalem, which were broken down, and the gates thereof were consumed with fire. Then I went on to the gate of the fountain, and to the king's pool: but there was no place for the beast that was under me to pass. Then went I up in the night by the brook, and viewed the wall, and turned back, and entered by the gate of the valley, and so returned. (Nehemiah 2:13–15)

Fasting and prayer must precede any spiritual restoration. Without that, Nehemiah would never have left Babylon to go rebuild the walls of Jerusalem. Likewise, if the church does not acknowledge her apostasy and repent, then God cannot restore her, because she would go right back to the condition that caused her apostasy in the first place.

> They said unto me, The remnant that are left of the captivity there in the province are in great affliction and reproach: the wall of Jerusalem also is broken down, and the gates thereof are burned with fire. And it came to pass, when I heard these words, that I sat down and wept, and mourned certain days, and fasted, and prayed before the God of heaven, And said, I beseech thee, O Lord God of heaven, the great and terrible God, that keepeth covenant and mercy for them that love him and observe his commandments: Let thine ear now be attentive, and thine eyes open, that thou mayest hear the prayer of thy

servant, which I pray before thee now, day and night, for the children of Israel thy servants, and confess the sins of the children of Israel, which we have sinned against thee. (Nehemiah 1:3–6)

Those believers who go through the slow process of falling into apostasy are rarely able to see it creeping into their church and are often in a denial that does not allow them to accept that their church is dying. The monotonous process of following our religious traditions cloaks the fact that we are slowly falling away. We can't see it because we aren't paying attention, and besides, it is too uncomfortable to think about. It is so much easier to listen to pied pipers who tell us God still loves us no matter what than to face the ugly truth that we have left the presence of God long ago and now are facing judgment.

We don't see it because we don't want to see it.

Dead Altars
Somewhere in this process of introspection, we must come to realize that no matter how much we love our church, if we are not winning souls we are not experiencing revival. As simple and obvious as that should be, coming to that realization is a major hurdle that keeps most churches from any supernatural move of God in their midst.

Jesus said that no man can come unto Him except the Father draws him (John 6:44). Using basic logic, if it is the Spirit of God that draws souls to repentance, and souls are not coming to your altar, then it stands to reason that God is not drawing them there. A church, especially its leadership, should ask themselves why.

Salt is the seasoning that makes food taste good. Jesus taught that we as believers are the salt of the earth, but if we have lost our savor, our taste, then we are good for nothing (Matthew 5:13). The world may be hungry for truth, but they don't want what we have to offer if it doesn't taste good. We need to give them a meal they want to come back for again and again.

Are your altars empty? Is there a lack of supernatural miracles and visitations in your church? Have your services become dry lectures about God with five bulleted points, a poem, and a couple of jokes? Is the power of the Holy Ghost no longer flowing through your services like a mighty rushing wind? Has it ever? Maybe it is time to come to grips with the fact that something is desperately wrong with your church. Something vital is missing in your walk with God, and you need to get it back. If you don't, instead of walking with Him you will find yourselves trudging along in aimless circles.

Of course, you may be completely satisfied with your church just the way it is. If that is the case, then you will get exactly what you desire. God will not push you any further than you want to go. If He does, you would never be able to handle the high price it would cost you, and you would never be able to nurture the babes in Christ that He would send you. He gave His life for those precious souls, and He will not hand them over to a people who do not care enough to also give their lives for them.

A church that is not winning souls is like the fig tree that had withered up and no longer produced fruit; it was a vine of dead branches. Jesus cursed the fig tree even when it was not in season (Matthew 21:19–21). There are no excuses you can offer that will deflect the judgment of God for not having fruit. There is never a time when winning souls is not in season.

A vine that does not bear forth fruit has to be cut off because it has become dead wood that can never come back to life (John 15:6). When the sap stops flowing through your church, it is dead and good for nothing but to be burned in the fire. When you no longer see souls getting saved, the sick healed, miracles and manifestations of the Holy Ghost performed, then maybe it is time to admit that your church is dead.

Over the last twelve years, I have preached to hundreds of churches across Africa, and almost all of the people in them expect the great white American evangelist to bless them with an encouraging message. I tell them, however, that I am not there so they can be blessed, get money, find a husband, or increase their crops. I am there to show them the truth of what God requires of them as believers in the gospel of Jesus Christ.

My first challenge to them is to ask if they believe they have a good church. If they are satisfied with their church and their Christian walk, then I need go no further. Let me find another congregation that is hungry for something more than just having church functions. As the saying goes, I am not looking for someone who is not looking; I am looking for those who are looking. The ones who are looking are those who are searching for the truth, whose hearts are broken for the lost, who are finished with "church as usual" and are desperately crying out for something more in God. They are hungry, desperate, and searching for God.

I challenge them by asking how many souls got saved in their church last week. How about last month? Okay, how about last year? This is the litmus test for Christianity. It doesn't matter how nice your church is, how wonderful your pastor is, or how much your members love each other. The question is, are you winning souls for Jesus Christ? Yes or no? Are you even trying? If you are not, then you are not fulfilling the call that God has placed on the church.

Every week many believers sit in the same seat in their church surrounded by the same faces. They tell each other the same nice things they told each other last week. They say they want revival, but they expect it to just fall out of the sky into their laps while they sit like dead wood on a wooden pew and do nothing. As the old adage says, if you do nothing, nothing will happen.

Some people simply don't care. They have church just the way they like it and resent any change. They don't want anything to upset the comfortable balance they currently enjoy. These are old wine bottles that cannot hold the new wine (Luke 5:36–39), the outpouring of the Holy Spirit that God is sending. These people will either have to burst, change, or leave in order for revival to come.

At some point you must acknowledge that something is missing and that the fire on your altars has gone out. The Spirit of God is no longer present, souls are not getting saved, and it doesn't look like there will be any new influx of sinners on their way to your altar anytime soon. Why should they? What have you got to offer them beyond timeworn expressions that have been repeated so many times that their original luster has turned dull and they no longer hold any real meaning to the unsaved.

Only when we acknowledge our failure can we turn our hearts to answer His call to revival.

Warnings from the Prophet Joel
The first chapter in the book of Joel describes the apostasy and revival that will occur just before the Second Coming of the Lord. It describes the time we are living in right now:

> That which the palmerworm hath left hath the locust eaten; and that which the locust hath left hath the cankerworm eaten; and that which the cankerworm hath left hath the caterpillar eaten. (Joel 1:4).

In the above scripture, Joel was describing how the fields of harvest, which symbolize the souls of the harvest, would be ruined by one predatory plague after another until there is nothing left. Our churches serve as threshing floors and barns to bring the harvest of new souls into.

Threshing floors serve as the place where the wheat is separated from the chaff, and barns are the place where the finished wheat is stored. In like manner, the church is the place where the spiritual wheat is saved from the chaff of the world and kept in the sanctuary of safety in the church. If the harvest is destroyed by these plagues, that would indicate that few souls would be getting saved. If revival is all about winning the lost, then this is a clear indication that something is terribly wrong with our churches.

In verse 5, the prophet calls to the vinedressers and the drinkers of wine, those who have been called to take care of the vine and fig tree of God, and tells them that the new wine would be cut off from their mouths and from the house of the Lord. If the new wine represents a new outpouring of the Spirit of God, then this would mean that the traditional church is going to miss this new outpouring of the Holy Spirit. Instead, Joel calls for a people that would be so hungry that they would strip the vine and the fig tree bare:

> A nation is come up upon my land, strong, and without number, whose teeth are the teeth of a lion, and he hath the cheek teeth of a great lion. He hath laid my vine waste, and barked my fig tree: he hath made it clean bare, and cast it away; the branches thereof are made white. (Joel 1:6–7)

Throughout the Bible, the fig tree and the vine are symbols of the Spirit and the Word of God, so this would be a group of people that are hungrier for God than any group before them. This group of people would be voracious readers of the Word of God and storm the altar of prayer. Joel referred again to that nation later on in the first half of chapter 2.

In verse 8, Joel calls for the church to "lament like a virgin for the husband of our youth." If we are the virgin bride of Christ, then this would be a sorrowful cry for us because something had gone terribly wrong with our relationship to the Lord. Like a virgin bride who has lost her beloved husband, this should cause the church to break out into serious cries. The Spirit of God has left and we are desolate and alone:

> The meat offering and the drink offering is cut off from the house of the Lord; the priests, the Lord's ministers, mourn. (Joel 1:9)

Here is what our cry should be cry about. We should be mourning for the loss of these two vitally essential services of the Lord: the meat offering and the drink offering. Notice that it is God who has cut them off, not us. Let's look at these two vitally important offerings and what they symbolize today.

The meat offering and the drink offering were part of the Continual Offering that is described in Exodus 29 and Numbers 28. This offering was required twice a day, every day. It is an analogy of our walk with God and our daily worship. Just as we are commanded to walk in righteousness before God and to keep His commandments, so is the perfect lamb, the sacrifice of our righteousness, upon the altar of our hearts. The fire on that altar is never supposed to go out, just as we are supposed to keep the fire in our hearts burning continuously.

The meat offering was fine flour mingled with pure beaten oil, a picture of the Word of God, which is the Bread of Life, anointed by the Holy Spirit, the pure oil beaten for purity. Paul wrote in 2 Corinthians 3:6 that the letter kills but the Spirit gives life. That oil is the anointing that gives the Word of God life. The drink offering was strong wine poured out before God, a picture of strong prayer. These two things must accompany your sacrifice of service and righteousness for it to be acceptable to God. Obviously, if they are taken away from the house of the Lord, there is great reason to mourn.

In the next verse, Joel cries that the Lord has gone even further in His judgment against the church:

> The field is wasted, the land mourneth; for the corn is wasted: the new wine is dried up, the oil languisheth. (Joel 1:10)

The field is the harvest field of souls (John 4:35). The Hebrew word for "wasted" is *shadad*, which means "to be ravaged and destroyed." If the fields are wasted, then this means the church is not winning souls, our altars are empty, the land mourns, and we are in desperate need of revival.

As a result of our dead altars, God has taken away the believers' ability to do three things: (1) to grasp depths of the Word of God (the corn), (2) to dive into a deeper vibrancy of prayer (the wine), and (3) to experience a greater anointing of the Holy Spirit (the oil).

The corn, or wheat, is the Word of God. Wheat makes flour which makes bread, and the Word of God is the Bread of Life. If the wheat is wasted or destroyed, then that means God has sealed the depths of the Word like He tells us in Isaiah:

> The vision of all is become unto you as the words of a book that is sealed, which men deliver to one that is learned, saying, Read this, I pray thee: and he saith, I cannot; for it is sealed. (Isaiah 29:11)

As we've said, when the wheat of the Bread of Life is wasted or sealed unto us, we can read it, but we are not able to receive the deeper understandings that come only through the Holy Spirit. It is sealed. The apostle Paul tells us that the Spirit is what gives life to the Word of God (2 Corinthians 3:6). Without the Spirit, the Bible is just a book and cannot affect the great changes that it can when it is charged with the Spirit. If the Word of God is "wasted," then so are we.

God has dried up the "new wine," our prayer life, communion in the Spirit through prayer with God. We pray, but that exciting anointing that sometimes comes down and lights up our prayer hour is the new wine that will be missing. There are many places in the Bible that wine is used as an analogy of the Spirit of God. Just as we can feel the effects of wine when we drink it, so also can we feel the effects of our communion with God when we drink of the Spirit of God in prayer.

The Hebrew word for "dried up" is *yabesh*, which means "to wither as someone who is ashamed." So when the wine is withered or dried up, so is our prayer life. Several times in the Old Testament, God refused to hear the cries of the Israelites because they had refused His calls to them to repent of their sin. If we will not do what He asks us to do, He will not do what we ask Him to do.

As evidence of this drying up of our prayer lives, I would point to the difference between the prayer lives of our generation and the prayer lives of those just a couple of generations ago. Back then, all-night prayer meetings were frequent, and believers prayed all night long. Today we are hard pressed to even find any all-night prayer meetings anymore, and when we do, they are only dished out into small individual portions so that everyone doesn't have to stay up all night together.

When that older generation prayed, they took it as a time of battle and would "pray it through" until they received an answer from the Lord. Today, most churches have lost the art of prayer. Few take prayer as a time of serious contending in the Spirit and spend the one, two, or three hours or whatever it takes to get that victory that you receive when you finally "break through" to the throne of God. Most Christians I talk to about this do not even know what I mean when I speak of these terms. For them, prayer is a time of convenience that is spent in polite conversational prayer. We have our "quiet time" with God, while our grandmothers were shaking the heavens and breaking down principalities. Why is there such a difference? Because the spirit of prayer, the new wine, has been dried up from the church and we no longer possess the power to pray like we once did.

The third thing that the prophet Joel tells us that God has done is to cause the oil to "languish." The oil is the anointing oil of the Holy Spirit. The Hebrew word for "languish" is *amal*, which means "to wax feeble." When the anointing oil languishes, or waxes feeble, then the miracles begin to disappear because it is only the Holy Spirit's power that performs those supernatural miracles.

Jesus told His disciples that signs will follow them that believe (Mark 16:17–18). That was one of the very last things He left them with so they would be encouraged to take the gospel to the rest of the world. Mark then related that, armed with that encouragement, they preached everywhere, confirming their words with signs following. Well here we are today. We have the same commission, the same faith, and the same God. Where, then, are the signs?

This is the same question Gideon asked: where are the signs? The Israelites of his generation had given themselves over to the enemy and had forgotten God. The Amalekites had taken over the land and destroyed the harvest, just as today our enemy of worldliness has infiltrated our churches and has destroyed the harvest of souls. Gideon was different, however. He sought the Lord in secret, and the Lord sent an angel to tell him he would deliver Israel. But he had this one piercing question:

> Oh my Lord, if the Lord be with us, why then is all this befallen us? and where be all his miracles which our fathers told us of, saying, Did not the Lord bring us up from Egypt? (Judges 6:13)

The absence of the supernatural indicates the absence of God. However you read it, it spells death for the church. The church is not in the place with God that she should be, and she badly needs revival.

In this same chapter 1 of Joel, the Lord called for the ministers of the Lord to cry out all night long and mourn because of the desolation of the church. The cattle, symbolizing the believers, would be groaning for pasture, wandering about searching for food, but would not be able to find any. The barns and garners, which are the churches where the harvest of souls should be brought into, are all broken down. Even the rivers of living water would be dried up.

In verse 16, we see that the meat, which is our spiritual sustenance, is cut off along with joy and gladness from the house of God. The joy of the Lord is our strength. If that joy is cut off from the house of the Lord, we are in deep trouble. There is no alternate interpretation.

This is specifically targeted to the Church in the last days. There are six places in Joel that specifically refer to the end times – Joel 1:15, 2:1, 2:10, 2:11, 2:31, and 3:41. This is not a prophesy for some other group of people in some other time – God is talking to us in this generation! He is cutting off the Spirit, the depths of the Word and prayer, the miracles and healings, and even the joy and gladness from the church in the last days. And you wonder why we see so few miracles?

He gives us the reason for all that desolation in verse 11:

> Be ye ashamed, O ye husbandmen; howl, O ye vinedressers, for the wheat and for the barley; because the harvest of the field is perished. (Joel 1:11)

Here is the most damning indictment against the church: the harvest of souls is perished and going to hell, and God blames us. We are the husbandmen that were supposed to bring the harvest into the house of the Lord. But are we ashamed? Hardly. We're too busy having church to even notice.

Amos said there would be a famine, not for bread and water, but for hearing the words of the Lord (Amos 8:11–13). Churches can be found everywhere in the United States, but we are not getting fed with the deep things of God. Oh, there are Bibles everywhere you look, but as Isaiah cried (29:11), the book is sealed to us; we read it, but our understanding barely skims the surface. The wheat, the real depth of the Word of God, is wasted and not available to us. We groan because of our hunger, but we do not know where to go for food because the entire spiritual landscape around us is wasted and barren.

If I were a blind invalid who had no knowledge of the world around me, this chapter in the book of Joel alone would be enough to convince me that the church in the last days had fallen from God. It would not be hard to believe that there would be little, if anything, left of the fertile fields of harvest that used to be flush with souls and a flowing of the Spirit of God. But we, like the people John wrote about, have eyes but cannot see and ears but cannot hear:

> He hath blinded their eyes, and hardened their heart; that they should not see with their eyes, nor understand with their heart, and be converted, and I should heal them. (John 12:40)

So much of our church world is dead, but we are so used to our apostasy that we do not have eyes to see it nor a heart to believe it even when the Holy Scriptures testify of it to our face.

Where Are the Miracles?
The same Spirit that draws lost souls to the altar is the same Spirit that heals the sick, raises the dead, and performs miracles. While it may seem easy to explain away your empty altars with religious and theological excuses, it is hard to deny the absence of the power of God to perform the miracles that the Bible says will follow them that believe. As we said, the prophet Joel declared that God would cut off the oil (the anointing oil of the Holy Spirit that performs the miracles). In other words, we are not seeing the miracles that come only through the Holy Spirit because the oil has been cut off.

Gideon, in Judges 6, was just a simple farmer, but he could see the desolation that had happened to Israel at the hands of their enemies. The Israelites had cried out to God for deliverance from their enemies who had taken over their land, but God answered that He had given them His law to keep but they had chosen the world instead. Because of that, He had allowed the enemy to come in and take over the land. So now Gideon had to thresh his wheat by the winepress in secret for fear the Amalekites would steal it. The threshing of wheat, which provides the Bread of Life, and the winepress of prayer, by which we seek the face of God, had to be done in secret. But it is in that secret place with God that prayers are answered.

The destruction of the fields of harvest that were taken over by the Amalekites is a damning testimony of what happens when the church compromises with the world. When we allow the world to come into the church, they will take over and they will destroy the harvest. Souls (the harvest) will no longer flock to our altars anymore. We end up weak and powerless before our enemies, unable to overcome weaknesses of the flesh, and strangers to the power of God. And we were the ones that let them in!

Gideon recognized the desolation for what it was while others were content to go along with the way things were, even building altars to Baal in a vain attempt to placate the enemy. While others were satisfied with a dead church, Gideon was not.

When an angel appeared to him and declared that Gideon was a "mighty man of valor," Gideon's response was a retort of desperation. "If God is with us, then where are the miracles?" (Judges 6:13) He knew that the absence of the supernatural indicated the absence of God.

Yeah. Good question. Where are the miracles? When's the last time you saw the sick healed, the dead raised, the outpouring of the Holy Ghost in your services, and souls flocking to the altar to get saved? If our churches are so good, then where did the Spirit of the Lord go? Where are the miracles?

Faith healings are rare because we don't expect them. In the very hands we raise to pray over the sick, we hold a doctor's appointment because we don't really believe God will heal us. We call it prudent, but God calls it unbelief. And don't you dare pray to raise the dead! That's considered extreme at best, crazy at worst. We, by our compliance with our spiritual desolation, hope for a peace that will never come from a compromise with the world. But men of God, like Gideon, see what is lacking and refuse to be satisfied without it.

The angel's answer to Gideon's cry about the absence of God's deliverance and the lack of miracles is telling: "Go in this thy might, and thou shalt save Israel" (Judges 6:14). What was that might, that strength? Gideon's strength was that he recognized their apostasy and their departure from God and was not willing to compromise with it.

The lack of miracles in our churches signifies a lack of the Spirit that produces them. And yet we are content to wallow in complacency rather than face the reality that the power of God has left us with an empty church whose walls of defense against the enemy have been broken-down.

Jesus' Last Request
When someone we love is about to pass away, we are deeply affected. As they pause at the door, about to cross the threshold of life, and turn to us with a last request, it is something we hold close to our heart. That last request is important. A dying father who gives his last request to his sons is able to die in peace knowing they will fulfill it.

As Jesus was about to leave this earth, the last thing He asked us to do for Him was to preach the gospel to the entire world. This last request is known as the Great Commission. It was the whole purpose for His death on the cross. Jesus died to save sinners from hell, and He left us with the job of finishing that task. There was no admonition to become learned scholars, prominent leaders of society, or ecclesiastical watchdogs. It was simple: win souls and make disciples. Deny yourself, pick up your cross, and follow Him. Follow Him where? To Golgotha, where He gave His life for the lost.

Have we chosen that same path, or have we meandered through the pathways of life that lead elsewhere? Have we convinced ourselves that we are fulfilling His last wish by attending church? Has fellowshipping with saints replaced going out to save sinners? As we are lifting up our hands in worship during a song service, secure in the belief that we are saved, are we content to limit the horizon of our vision for God to the church walls? When we turn our attention inward and lose sight of those outside, we lose our grasp on the purpose of our own salvation. When a church will not look beyond its walls, it denies its very reason for existence.

We did not get saved for ourselves. If the whole reason for your salvation was so you could go to heaven, then why not just get saved and keel over and die? Why hang around? You're just wasting the air. Why stay here in this world? Just go. Go to heaven and be done with it!

Ah, but you didn't die, did you? Perhaps it is about something more than your own salvation. Perhaps we have received this gift of salvation so we could pass it on to others. Why else would we still be here?

When our altars are bare, we are ignoring the last request of our Savior who gave His life for these souls that we have dismissed.

Charity, the Secret to Revival

Often I hear people who are quick to justify their church's lack of power by pointing to all the good works they do. They have canned food drives for the poor, lead children's toy drives at Christmas, and volunteer for community causes. They're all good things but not the signs of revival.

There are lots of good works we can do, and should do, as the church of Jesus Christ. The unsaved also do those things, but that doesn't mean they are filled with the Spirit of God. Charity, real charity, is more than good works. Charity is the giving of oneself out of love so souls can be saved. It is the very essence of Christianity, the real meaning of the cross. The ultimate focus of charity is to win souls and nurture them. When true charity is present in a church, the members will bring in the lost to hear the gospel. When it is absent, no one is cut to the heart or burdened for the lost, and the altars remain empty.

Jesus commanded us to invite not only our friends to our feasts but also the sick, the maimed, and the poor (Luke 14:13). When most of us gaze around at our congregation, however, all we see are the same old faces we see every week. We have our feast and have invited our friends, but we have not sought out the blind, the maimed, and the poor like Jesus told us to do. If that is the case with your church, then there is a definite lack of charity present, and certainly no revival.

The prophet Amos painted a picture of a people who are comfortable and at ease, enjoying the blessings of life, but who are not grieving for the lost (Amos 6:1–7). They lay on their beds of ivory but are not grieved for the affliction of their people. According to verse 7, they will be the first who will feel the sting of judgment, because judgment must begin at the house of God. This is not just a matter of choices without consequences. If you are not moved by charity to seek and save the lost, to ignite your church and start the sap flowing again from the True Vine, then you will face the wrath of God because you did not care about the souls He gave His life to save.

Charity is about winning the lost. Jesus was Charity incarnate and He came to save sinners. It was what He died on the cross for. Charity, therefore, is more than feelings and emotions; it is about action. Paul told the Corinthians that you can abound in all kinds of spiritual gifts—prophecy, wisdom and faith—but if you do not have charity, you are nothing (1 Corinthians 13:2). The essence of charity is wrapped up in the drive to save souls.

What will it take to bring you to a realization that something is missing in your church? Churches in America have been so long without a true revival that we ignore the blatant signs of our death and settle for excuses that measure us up with other dead churches to convince us that we are normal.

If all you want is to be what the world calls "normal" and take an easy route to complacent Christianity, then you will never experience the power of God in your life. But if you want to experience the vibrancy and fullness of the power of God, you must first come to grips with the reality that your church is not experiencing revival.

Only then can you see something so supernatural happen that it will be spoken about throughout eternity.

A Barren Woman
Throughout the Bible, the institution of marriage is presented as a picture of the believer's relationship with God. Jesus Christ is the Bridegroom; His church is the bride. Everything from the courtship to the kids has its analogy in our relationship with Him. It's as if God has given us this picture in living color, the most important of all our relationships here on earth, as a constant and vibrant reminder of what life is really all about. Marriage is not just about sex. Neither is it only about taking care of one another, keeping the house clean and making the bed, cooking the food, or taking out the trash. All those things have their analogy in our walk with God, but the primary purpose of marriage is to be fruitful and multiply and fill the earth with fruit. God gave this instruction to many in the Old Testament, including Adam, Noah, Abraham, and Jacob.

As mentioned in chapter 2, when a wife was barren in the Old Testament, it was considered a shame to her. Today, of course, with our many career-minded women, raising a family does not take on the same importance as it did originally. But regardless of its application today, the picture still remains clear: the wife was to bear children and make raising them her priority. That same charge is placed on the church, the Bride of Christ, in the spiritual realm.

I have listened to some Christians excuse themselves from soul winning by saying that the fruit we are charged with bearing are really just the fruit of the Spirit (Galatians 5:22). I disagree. That fruit is the result of the Holy Spirit working in believers, not a charge put on us to fulfill. The Great Commission is not asking us to develop good characteristics, but to go out and win souls. The simplicity of the gospel is easily turned into complex excuses when we refuse to surrender our own comfortable ways of life and step out to obey the call of God.

Two wonderful examples of the godly desire to bring forth fruit can be seen in two women in the Old Testament. Hannah and Rachael were both barren women who offered vows to God to escape the shame of a fruitless marriage. The shame was real to them, even though both were the favored wives of their husbands. For them their purpose in life was not to receive love from their spouse but to have children. The issue of childlessness was not that it would reflect on their personal value but that it would affect their husband's honor. So we should honor Christ by winning souls and raising them in Him.

The church today is a barren woman. It does not matter how pretty she is, how wealthy she is, or how many skills she has mastered. If the church is not winning souls, she is a barren woman. We seem to be able to erect great edifices to show the prosperity and livelihood of our church, but we spend little time searching for souls to fill them. It is much easier to build fitness centers and Christian coffeehouses than it is to witness face-to-face to the unsaved. It is our way out of controversy. We hope we can still be a witness without the difficulty of exposing ourselves to any individual embarrassment.

Is that not true? Can you not see it all around you? When is the last time you or your church actually took to the streets to witness to strangers and tell them about salvation? And yet Jesus' command is clear to go out to the highways and compel them to come in to your Father's house so that the marriage supper of the Lamb may be filled (Luke 14:23). What is it that is stopping you from keeping this commandment? If it is the fear of man, then you do not fear God. If it is embarrassment, then you do not have a strong enough love for the lost. If it is too many social commitments, then you are too tied to this world. If you think you have a better idea on how to win souls, then you need to learn that you cannot figure out your way to heaven. It is a simple matter of trust and obey. Remember, obedience is better than sacrifice, but rebellion is as the sin of witchcraft (1 Samuel 15:23).

I believe the biggest thing that holds us back from being effective witnesses is our lack of enthusiasm. We don't possess that fire of excitement that will drive us without any regard for embarrassment to tell strangers about the wonderful things that God is doing in our church and what He can do for them.

Laziness and Resistance to Change
Many people simply do not like change. Once they organize things the way they think they should be, they will defend them ferociously. A lot of folks like the feel of constricted walls around them to feel safe. Any breach of that security threatens the way they have everything organized in their minds. They just have too much trouble walking without solid ground under their feet, so it is easier to stick with the liturgical traditions they are used to than to break into something that seems untested and revolutionary. They are stuck in "church as usual," and are old wine bottles that cannot stretch with the new wine.

The problem is, the foundations they are built on are based on the wrong premise. Religion is the carnal representation of our spiritual walk with God, but if we grab onto the carnal to secure the spiritual, we will find ourselves with a handful of sand. Faith is the evidence of things *not* seen, and it is the substance of things hoped for (Hebrews 11:1). If your hope is anchored on things you can see because you are not able take hold of what you cannot see, then it will be difficult for you to embrace a supernatural change in your church.

Let's look at the story of Lazarus (John 11:1–46) and how it relates to being bound by religious traditions. Lazarus had died, but when Jesus arrived, He called Lazarus forth out of a stone tomb, bound hand and foot in the graveclothes of religious tradition. His face was also bound with a napkin so he couldn't see. Jesus had the stone rolled away and called Lazarus to come forth out of the tomb, but He then commanded His disciples to loose him from those grave clothes and set him free. It takes the hand of God to roll away that stone and call the church forth to the light, but it is His disciples who are commanded to loose the church from the rotting tradition that binds her. We have to hold these people up in prayer, because only God can reassure them to let go of the leatherlike stiffness of old traditions.

There are other believers who are simply too lazy to want revival. Any fool will know that seeking revival is spelled W-O-R-K, but some people just don't care to stretch themselves that far. They don't mind if someone else does the work, but don't ask them to crucify their flesh, especially for someone whom they have never met. They don't mind praying, but not all night long, especially when it isn't for themselves. They don't mind witnessing as long it's to someone who is already saved and agrees with them, but don't ask them to go out into the highways and byways to witness to the lost. They are holding on to a vicarious salvation that assumes they can latch on to the coattails of their pastor to carry them to heaven. But while you can hide on a bench in the back of the church, you will not hide at the judgment bar of God.

When I was very young in the Lord, I asked Him why some people get saved and some people do not; why some people stay saved, and why others fall away. He spoke directly to me: *Some people care, and some people do not. It's as simple as that.*

That was one of the most profound things I have ever heard. Water seeks its own level. Anyone can recognize the need, but if we don't really care, we will always settle back to that level where we are comfortable. If we want a revival, however, we will have to care enough to drive ourselves past our own fleshly desires. If we try to rise above our own level of passion without the Spirit of God igniting our hearts, it will not be long before we settle back to that same level where we are comfortable. Only God can give us that drive, and it is to Him that we look for the passion to break out of our complacency.

But we have to ask for it.

It is written that if a son asks his father for a loaf of bread, will he give him a stone? How much more will your heavenly Father give the Spirit to them that ask Him? (Luke 11:11). Our sin, therefore, will be that we didn't care enough to ask, and ask earnestly enough. If we did, surely God would give us the desire and the power to carry the burden He has asked us to carry.

Just as the father of the child with the unclean spirit begged Jesus to help his unbelief (Mark 9:24), so may we plead with God to place an enduring and passionate desire in our hearts for revival. We may only be flesh, but God can place that strong burden for revival, for holiness, and for lost souls on our hearts that will make us what we are not. If we do not pray for that burden, it will not be long before we fall back to our own level again.

While the first step to revival is merely a matter of facing facts, I believe that seeking God for the desire for revival is the first test we must pass. You have to want revival so badly that you are desperate for it. There cannot be any alternative for you, and no back door excuses if it does not come. Your soul has to be wrenched from its slumber with a passionate fire that will not stop burning until revival comes. Only God can give that to you. It does not come naturally; it is only by the grace of God. Therefore, we have to seek the face of God for it. We have to make a choice to start the whole process by asking God to help our infirmities and set our hearts on fire. If we are serious, we will continue in prayer until we get it. If we give up before the answer, then we fall short of the calling He has placed on us, and we choose to fail not only God but ourselves and the countless souls of others who would have come to salvation through us.

God will not send His precious souls to a church that doesn't care enough to fast and pray for them. If He did, they would soon die, because no one would take the burden upon themselves to water them, nurture them, and help keep their fires burning. But if the people in a church have a burning desire to break their spirits, die to themselves, and seek the face of God for souls, then when God sends those souls, they will value them as a precious gift they have labored for.

When we overcome our laziness and the dimness of our own sight to stretch our vision past our horizons, we will find a God who has been patiently waiting for us to believe Him for the supernatural. These are the faithful souls whom God can use to bring revival. The faint, the unbelieving, and the fearful will never climb high enough to look over Mount Pisgah to see the promised land of revival. We rise to the challenge of God only by His grace so that when it is all said and done, it is God alone who gets all the glory.

Rachel's Cry
It is one thing to realize you do not have a revival burning in your church, but it is an entirely different thing to want one. It may seem that these two things would naturally go together, but they do not.

Wanting children so badly, Rachel prayed:

> When Rachel saw that she bare Jacob no children, Rachel envied her sister; and said unto Jacob, Give me children, or else I die. (Genesis 30:1)

Rachel was not asking for a blessing for herself; she was desperate for souls. This is where most of us miss it. Our great underlying purpose in life is not about us; it's about others. This is not about revival for revival's sake or a move of God so we can feel good about ourselves. It is a deep conviction in our hearts that souls are going to spend eternity in hell if we don't do something to stop it.

Are you desperate for revival? Like Rachel, do you want it badly enough to die for it, to give your life to see souls get saved? Anything less than that is like a sounding brass or a tinkling cymbal: lots of noise but no substance. Or as Peter describes it, as wells without water and clouds without rain (2 Peter 2:17). We say we want revival in our churches because we know we're supposed to, but how badly do we really want it? The price of true revival is higher than what human flesh wants to pay. It takes the Spirit of the Lord to bring us to that place of selfless passion that will drive us past our comfort zone to take upon ourselves the suffering of the body of Christ that the Word of God calls us to.

This is not a mindless suffering for suffering's sake but a commitment to offer ourselves, both spiritually and physically, to see the ultimate cause of Christ reign victorious. In the book of Revelation, God does not admonish us that those who <u>try</u> will eat of the Tree of Life but those who <u>overcome</u>. The greatest obstacle we face is our own fleshly desires. We have to reach past what is normal and comfortable and enter into a walk with God that has crucified those fleshly desires so we can walk in the Spirit of God. This is the challenge that God sets before us to test our determination. It separates the sheep from the goats and raises the real men and women of God from the ranks of mediocrity.

5
Step 2 Repentance

If my people, which are called by my name, shall humble themselves, and pray, and seek my face, and turn from their wicked ways; then will I hear from heaven, and will forgive their sin, and will heal their land. (2 Chronicles 7:14)

THIS HEAVILY QUOTED scripture is touted as a banner cry for revival, but in order to bring our land to this point, someone has to get on their knees. It has to start somewhere. No revival comes without repentance.

The Call to Individual Holiness
Every revival in history has been preceded by a time of deep, heart-rending repentance that leads to extreme holiness throughout the church. Before the move of God can begin to work in the church, it must find a clean and holy foundation to stand upon. If we are looking for a supernatural move of God, our temple must be scoured from sin to accept His presence. God will not fellowship with sin.

This kind of repentance cannot be faked. You cannot mouth the words because you think that's what you are supposed to do or even want to do. It has to be a sincere, deep flood of repentance that issues from the very depths of your soul. This is not the flippant requests we shoot up to God for a quick fix to patch something stupid we have done. This is like no other deep cry for forgiveness that we have ever experienced, and it must be real if it is to reach a holy God's ears.

Paul warned us about the seriousness of sin:

> For if we sin wilfully after that we have received the knowledge of the truth, there remaineth no more sacrifice for sins, But a certain fearful looking for of judgment and fiery indignation, which shall devour the adversaries (Hebrews 10:26–27).

We cannot rest on our initial salvation experience. Our lives must show a continued walk in holiness before God, and our failures must show up in stark contrast to that holiness. These shortcomings in our lives must be brought to the light of God's judgment and mercy to be completely cleansed and forgiven before our vessels can be made ready and "meet for the Master's use" (2 Timothy 2:21).

When a true repentance like that takes over the church, seemingly harmless sins will become glaringly wicked as they stand in contrast to the holiness of the Lord God Almighty. The closer the presence of the Lord comes, the darker those sins appear until His blinding light exposes every dark corner of our hearts. We soon feel the weight of our sins so heavily that we cannot keep our knees from crashing to the floor in prayer for forgiveness like we have never known before.

I have seen Christians in revival services like that when Holy Ghost conviction takes over, sobbing uncontrollably for things that the day before had seemed nothing more than just a normal part of life. God's light is blinding, and even the slightest darkness stands in sharp contrast. No longer could they stand the separation from God that these things caused them. The guilt became so heavy that they had to repent in the most strident cries of the heart, confessing out loud to the whole congregation the things they had never even considered before as being wrong.

There is something about this kind of deep confession that is so cleansing that it fills people with a joy of relief that shines out from their faces. Breaking those secret shackles brings a freedom that most have never felt before, and a weight falls off them that they hadn't realized they'd been carrying for so long. It is liberating. It's as if they can't wait to tell everyone, and they no longer care what anyone thinks. They are free!

Without that freedom of sanctification, God cannot move. If we are not holy, the move of God will be mired down in the layer of mud that covers our souls. Under the Levitical law, the altar first had to be sanctified by blood before it could be holy enough to accept sacrifices to the Lord. Once all sin has been swept out of the church and all the stale air of mediocrity is blown out the windows, the altar is now sanctified and the sanctuary cleansed. Now, and only now, can God inhabit the church in complete holiness and prepare the unhampered offering of ourselves to Him in worship.

That freedom from every shadow of sin lends boldness and a newly found strength of faith to the believer. Because the righteous are as bold as lions (Proverbs 28:1), this extreme holiness now raises up ferocious faith in men and women who have the holy boldness to march right into the throne room itself, roaring in a warrior faith to demand their rights to the throne of God. These are not timid sheep afraid to bother their Master but warriors of God who stand in righteousness to grab hold of the horns of the altar and claim the promises of God and will not let go until God moves.

It is with such faith that God is well pleased and is bound by His own Word to respond to this kind of call for revival. He *has* to answer because of their severe righteousness, and the men and women who have entered into this level of faith know it and will not be denied.

Repentance brings righteousness, and righteousness liberates faith, and faith moves mountains. Now we can stand before God and claim the fullness of His promises to us and know that because we are righteous before Him, He has to answer us. Revival is on the way. We know it. We claim it. We now have the faith to believe Him for it. It will come.

Righteousness establishes the promises of God.

Corporate Repentance

Personal repentance builds the foundation for corporate repentance. With the clarity that comes from a renewed personal relationship with God, it is easy to see how far our failings have taken us. We now realize how much not only we but our entire nation, our churches, and our people have been separated from God. Things that seemed normal or at least passable before are now colored in shades of darkness that can only be seen from the brightness of His light. We wonder how we never saw this before, but it is because we got used to the twilight creeping into our churches over time.

If we want a revival that will reach past our church doors, we have to beseech God to bring that same forgiveness to our entire land. The specter of apostasy hangs over our nation like a dark cloud, and we must pray for God's forgiveness for us all.

The key here is the realization that we used to be just like the people who we now see as unenlightened. Many of our neighbors, our countrymen, and the stalwart members of our churches maintain a diligence in attendance to what we now see as somber halls of religion. They need the same experience of repentance that we have just had. Our burden for lost souls begins here. Our heart has to break for those who are laboring under the same blankets of apostasy that we just came out of.

Jesus called Lazarus out of the tomb, but He called to His disciples to loose him from the graveclothes of old religious traditions (John 11:43). So we also are called to intercede for the church. Looking past the denominational differences, we are called to pray one for another. When revival comes, it has no affiliations.

Judgment will begin at the house of God, and so should our prayers for mercy.

Daniel's Prayer of Repentance

The story of the restoration of Jerusalem is one of the greatest and most detailed accounts of revival in the Bible. Space does not allow for recounting the fall of Israel, the pleading of the prophets, and the judgments of God, but suffice it to say, in every judgment of God there are always the seeds of the next revival. Daniel was one of those seeds:

> In the first year of his reign I Daniel understood by books the number of the years, whereof the word of the Lord came to Jeremiah the prophet, that he would accomplish seventy years in the desolations of Jerusalem. And I set my face unto the Lord God, to seek by prayer and supplications, with fasting, and sackcloth, and ashes. (Daniel 9:2–3)

Isaiah, who set the stage for Cyrus to issue the decree, also was a seed of revival. Esther was another seed who encouraged Artaxerxes to confirm the decree to restore Jerusalem, along with Nehemiah, Ezra, and others. The prophecy was written, the stage was set, the seeds were planted, but it was Daniel who prayed it in.

When you read a word from God right in the Holy Scriptures, you know that it is true. It is written; God said it; it must come to pass. Daniel read in the book of Jeremiah that the Babylonian captivity would last seventy years and then God would restore Israel to Jerusalem. The children of Israel had strayed far from the righteousness of God and had become slaves in Babylon as a result of their rebellion, but here was a revelation of the incredible mercy of God! The seventy years were about to be up, and Daniel knew restoration was coming. Revival was coming because God said so!

Although it was written in the Word of God and the time for this revival was upon them, did Daniel call his friends to sing and rejoice? Did they celebrate this new hope of restoration? No, Daniel was one of the wisest men that ever lived, and he knew that even though it had been prophesied in God's Word, without repentance there would be no revival.

To partake of this wonderful call back to God's grace, repentance had to be sought, not just individually, but corporately, for the whole body of the people of God.

Somebody had to get on their knees, and Daniel was the man. His prayer for forgiveness for his people is one of the longest prayers in the Old Testament (Daniel 9).

E. M. Bounds, a well-respected author of books on prayer, once wrote that God will not do anything *without* prayer that He can do *with* prayer. How true. God could do it all, but He doesn't. He uses flesh. We are His body, the arms and legs of the gospel here on earth. It is our faith that moves mountains and our prayers that move God. God's plan is for us to be the instruments of His mercy and to follow the example of His Son, Jesus Christ.

As we seek the face of God in repentance for our people, we remove the curse and open the door to allow the restoration to begin. Prayer unties the hands of God

Nehemiah

Nehemiah also knew the importance of repentance in birthing a revival. He wept as he heard how Jerusalem lay in ruins. This was the city of God. It was supposed to be beautiful and built as a monument to the glory of God, but it was destroyed because of the sins of his people, the people of God. Nehemiah's heart was broken.

Nehemiah was the king's cupbearer, whose function was to taste and make sure the wine, which held so much importance in that society, was not only safe but tasted good. A cupbearer for royalty was a position of great responsibility, power, and honor and would of necessity be someone who was well-trusted. As the king's cupbearer, he had access to the one who could issue the command to rebuild the city, but even so, he also knew that without repentance to God for the sins of the people that had caused this destruction, his request would be in vain. Day and night, Nehemiah fasted and prayed for God to forgive his people and grant him favor as he brought his supplication before the king.

That is serious prayer—day and night, fasting for days on end, desperate for an answer from God. There are times when you cannot afford to settle for a "maybe" from God. When you absolutely *have* to get an answer from God, then you will set aside the flesh and anything else that gets in the way and set yourself before Him alone who can deliver you. And then you stay there until the answer comes. Nehemiah knew that for the sake of his people who were perishing in slavery, he had to get an answer. There was no other option.

We, the called of Jesus Christ, are our King's cupbearers because we bear the wine of the Spirit of God in our capacity to serve our King. Like Nehemiah, we sit in spiritual captivity in a pagan land while the church lies in spiritual ruins. The walls of salvation are broken down and the church is in ruins, leaving the church defenseless against the enemy. Like Nehemiah and Daniel, we must acknowledge the cause of our current state and cry out to God for forgiveness for our nation and our churches.

If we do not address this, how can God reverse His judgments? If we do not acknowledge this sincerely brokenhearted, how can we expect God to hear from heaven and forgive us? Our people would soon return to the same carnal religious ways they were in before.

This is a test of a Christian's heart. Are we truly sorry for our sin? Do we lament and mourn for a return to God to the point that we are willing to pray and fast day and night? Do we agonize over the sins and failures of our people and cry out to God with all our hearts for Him to have mercy on His people? While the judgment of God is sure, there is also mercy if our hearts are sincere, and we can turn the wrath of God with a repentance that will pierce the heavens and reach His throne.

Halfhearted prayers will not do. We must be broken before God can restore us. He cannot fill a vessel that has not first been emptied through repentance.

Elijah's Challenge
In 1 Kings 18 we read the story of Elijah's challenge on Mount Carmel. Elijah called down fire in the midst of the children of Israel who had wholly turned to worship Baal, but when the fire fell, did it bring

forth a revival? Hardly. "The Lord, he is the God; the Lord, he is the God" (verse 39), the children of Israel called out, but acknowledgment does not constitute repentance. They were willing to stand by while their local priests were slaughtered in a cleansing action at the brook Kishon (verse 40), but they were not willing to fall to their knees in brokenhearted sorrow for their sin. They were more concerned about their own lives than the life of their church. There was no corporate repentance to break up the fallow ground of the nation.

Elijah had no revival or restoration to the house of God, and neither did his successor, Elisha. It takes a corporate repentance to revive the corporate body, and that would not come until years later. Even though the prophet was a true man of God, the fallow ground of Israel's heart had not been broken up to receive the seed of the Word of God, and so no harvest would be able to spring out of that hard, dry ground. Brokenhearted repentance is the only thing that can break up that fallow ground, watered by our tears, so that the seeds of God's Word can find soil to bring the harvest of revival.

Why are we so blind to spiritual realities? Why is it so hard to break our hearts to come to that broken repentance that God requires? Desire mixed with adversity and oppression will only make us sorry. Somewhere in that mix must be a hunger for righteousness, a longing for something other than what this world has to offer in comfort and prosperity. I honestly believe that the people on top of Mount Carmel had more of a desire to return to a life of prosperity than to a life of holiness. Their hearts were not broken with their sin; they merely recognized their mistake.

There are two separate worlds around us: the natural world we see around us and the spiritual world of eternity. The more we are in one, the less we are in the other. Until a hunger for holiness rises in our hearts, the comforts of this world blind us from seeing beyond our everyday lives. King Solomon wrote: "Where there is no vision, the people perish" (Proverbs 29:18). We have to be able to look beyond Mount Carmel and see the Beulah Land that is afar off and yearn for it as our only home. Only when we reach past the veil of this world to grasp the substance of things hoped for, can we ever truly relinquish our hold on the carnal world and find a true place of repentance.

Desire for righteousness exposes our need for repentance, not only for ourselves but for our nation and our churches. When that happens, we will willingly break up the fallow ground of our hearts to plant the seeds of revival. It takes time and a determined heart that will not settle for anything less, no matter how long it takes. No substitute will do, no matter how nice your church is. Only a genuine revival that is straight from the altar of God will satisfy the longing that God has put in His servants' hearts.

That is why Nehemiah prayed so hard to see the church restored. He had to have the real thing. That is why Elijah put his life on the line, why Daniel crashed to his knees, and why those who are touched with Rachel's cry of "give me souls lest I die," will contend in fasting and prayer until God answers.

Until that mercy is obtained, there can be no revival.

The Failure of the Church to Win Souls
Before we fall to our knees in repentance, we should know what we are repenting of. The repentance that the prophet Joel called for is one that will "rend your heart, and not your garments" (Joel 2:13). True repentance has to issue forth from the bottom of a broken heart or it is merely a form of hypocrisy. But in order to reach the sincerity of heartfelt repentance that is needed, we have to know what it is that is so wrong. Is it that we just haven't had good enough "church"? Or we haven't sung loudly enough? Or we weren't nice enough? What is the heart of the problem? What do we need to repent of?

Our greatest sin, which has caused the spiritual dearth that Joel prophesied would come upon the church in the last days, is our failure to bring the gospel to the lost. We have allowed the harvest of souls to perish (Joel 1:11).

Winning souls is not just another function of the church, something we do when we have extra time or something that is relegated to the leadership of the church to perform. This is not something on the same level as having a canned food drive, gathering toys to give out to the poor for Christmas, or organizing a blood drive. Winning souls is the very essence of the call of Christ; it is the very heartbeat of God. It is what you were called to do when you got saved. It is one of the two primary functions of the church. Jesus said that He would we bear much fruit, and that our fruit would remain (John 15:16). But before your fruit can remain, we must first go out and win them to the Lord.

I find in most churches that people have a tendency to believe that if they just support their church, somehow that will translate into new people coming in to get saved. They leave the burden and the worry of that to their pastors. After all, isn't that what pastors get paid to do? My retort is that shepherds don't give birth to sheep; sheep give birth to sheep. God places the responsibility to witness to the lost firmly at the feet of us all. And He makes it clear that it is not something we should do only when it is convenient. Our very place in God is at stake here. This is not *a* thing to do; it is *the* thing to do.

If the primary reason for God to send revival is to win the lost, then that is where we should turn our attention. Few of us realize how utterly important soul winning is to God. This is the heart of the problem. We have to take our focus off ourselves and turn it to others.

God is counting on us to be His witnesses on earth, and He said, "I have declared, and have saved, and I have showed, when there was no strange god among you: therefore ye are my witnesses, saith the Lord, that I am God" (Isaiah 43:12). This is what is broken in the church. To fix it, we must start with our deepest repentance to the throne of God.

6
Step 3 How to Build a Fire in the Church

IT'S EASY TO spout off a bunch of high-sounding rhetoric that promotes admirable goals, but without a clear understanding of just how we will achieve those goals, we are left wandering around without direction. Before long, with our zeal exasperated, we would settle back down into the mediocrity that we just came out of. We need a fire in the church to set us burning.

Before we can set a fire in the world, there has to be a fire in our church. If there is no fire there, the unsaved will turn around and head back into the world. Why should they stay? What do you have to offer them besides your philosophy about God? We have to have something to offer them that they want.

When a fire is burning in the church, it will give us the driving compulsion to share the excitement with everyone. Without it, we are merely going through the motions of doing what we feel we are supposed to do. We need a fire that burns so hot that it ignites us. That is what revival does. It sets us on fire so we can set the church on fire so the church can set the world on fire.

We need to create an excitement that will drive us with passion and continue to grow and spread out into our community. Where do we get the drive, desire, passion, and zeal to push past the reluctance of our flesh to accomplish these things? How do we build a fire in the church that will spread throughout our community and create the excitement that brings revival?

Jesus said we are the salt of the earth (Matthew 5:13); we are the savor that salts the meal that we offer to the world. Our salt is supposed to make that meal taste so good to the unsaved that they will want more. But if our salt has lost its savor, it is good for nothing. If we bring the unsaved into a church that does not have a fire burning in it, if the salt has no taste to it, then they will turn around and walk back out. If you have nothing more to offer them than what they can already get out in the world, then why should they surrender their lives to your dead religion?

The gospel of Jesus Christ is not some dead philosophy about God or some intelligent idea with a new perspective on life and eternity. It is the *power* of God unto salvation (Romans 1:16). If you have nothing more to offer than a dead religion and a gospel that has no power, then you have nothing to offer unsaved souls that are hungry for truth. We need power in our messages and fire in our churches. All the theological knowledge in the world will not do any good without it. When there is a fire burning in the church, however, everything happens naturally. The excitement rises in each of the members of the congregation until they find themselves racing out into their community to tell others what is happening in their church. Their neighbors can see it in their eyes and hear it in their voices, and the excitement begins to spread. Like a fire in a field of grass, once it catches hold, the fire cannot be stopped.

The only thing that will start a fire is another fire. Understanding that makes it easy to see that to build a fire in the church we need to first build a fire in the individuals *in* the church. The heat from any fire burns up, not down. A fire in the pulpit will only bring conviction. The fire needs to start in the pews, and from there it will spread among the congregation, and then it will set the rest of the church on fire.

How do we do that? The simplest answer I can give is that everything about serving the Lord always comes down to the same two things: the Word of God and prayer. But it begins with the Word because the Word of God is the source of all power. It is the Word of God that created the entire universe, and it is the Word of God that will bring revival so that, in the end, it will be God who gets the glory, not man.

To build a fire, you need both fuel and a spark. The Word of God is the wood and prayer is the spark. Either, alone, will not burn, but put them together, and you will start a fire.

The Word gives us knowledge and understanding. It gives us wisdom in the fear of the Lord and discernment in spiritual things (Proverbs 1). It washes us from uncleanness and gives us power over sin (Psalm 119:9). It gives us light to see (Psalm 119:105) and ears to hear, but most importantly, it gives us the power to pray.

If you are going to pray, you have to believe that God will hear you; otherwise it will do you no good, because without faith it's impossible to please God (Hebrews 11:6). And where do you get faith? It comes from hearing the Word of God (Romans 10:17). So it is the Word of God that gives us the faith to be able to pray.

When you take the faith you gained through reading the Word of God to the throne of God in prayer, the Spirit of God will come down as you pray. When you take that Spirit you just received in prayer back to the Word of God, you will go deeper, because the Spirit and the Word agree as one (1 John 5:7). When you go deeper, your ears will open even more and you'll increase your faith. You take that increased faith back to prayer and you will go higher. When you go higher, you will get more of the Spirit. Take that Spirit back to the Word again, and you will go even deeper. And then higher, and then deeper, and higher, and deeper, and on and on until a fire begins to blaze in your heart and sets you on fire! That's how it is done! There is no other way.

Once you are on fire, you will set others on fire, and they will set even more people on fire, and it will spread like wildfire in your church. When your church is on fire, it will spread that fire throughout your community. And when your community is on fire, it will keep on burning until revival falls out of the sky. And then nothing can stop it.

But it all starts with reading the Word of God.

The Wedding at Cana

In the story of the wedding at Cana (John 2), God has left us specific instructions about how to bring a move of the Spirit to the church. Jesus and His disciples were invited to a wedding feast where the host had run out of wine. The wedding feast is a picture of the church, and wine is symbolic of the Spirit, so a wedding feast without wine is like a church without the Spirit of God in it.

Mary, knowing her Son, told the servants in a specific, authoritarian tone, "Whatsoever he saith unto you, *do it!*" (verse 5, my emphasis). Want revival? Then whatever He tells you to do, do it.

What did Jesus tell them to do? He said, "Fill the waterpots with water" (verse 7).

Water is symbolic of the Word of God. We see this in the passage that speaks of the washing of the water by the Word (Ephesians 5:26). We see it in the rock that brought forth water (Deuteronomy 8:15), in the laver of brass in the tabernacle (Exodus 30:18), and in many other places.

Also to be noted is that there were six waterpots of stone or clay (John 2:6). Six is the biblical number associated with man (Revelation 13:18 is just one example). Also, just as God is the Potter and we are the clay, so do these clay waterpots represent the people in the church.

In the story, Jesus told the servants to fill the waterpots with water. They filled them, not half way or most of the way, but to the brim (verse 7)! When the water was poured out to the governor of the feast, the water turned to wine.

So what was Jesus telling us to do? Fill the people in the church all the way up to the brim with the water of the Word of God, not halfway or almost full, but all the way up to the brim! When the waterpots are filled all the way to the brim, the Spirit and the Word will agree (1 John 5:7–8), and the water of the Word of God turns to the wine of the Holy Spirit!

Can there be any instructions more specific? Do we not understand that all power emanates from the Word of God and nowhere else? When that power from the Word is channeled through prayer, it will start a fire. It does not come from books, seminars, videos, singing, or dancing; not from holding a good thought nor any other human endeavor or substitute. The fire comes only from the Word of God that framed the worlds, created the universe, brought life into existence, and then was made flesh and went to the cross to shed blood for our atonement and sanctification. You cannot do it any other way, because there is no other power that can bring forth revival in your church. Jesus said that without Him, we can do nothing (John 15:5), and He *is* the Word of God.

You want a fire in your church? Read the Word of God. Read and read and read and read until you are filled to the brim with the power of the Word of God, and then go pour out the wine to the governor of the feast.

No excuses. No substitutes. No other way.

Elijah on Mount Carmel
Elijah had been called by God as a prophet during a time of plenty. With green fields and flowing rivers all around him, he stood before King Ahab of Israel, and declared the end of the rain. Everyone laughed him to scorn, but three years later, no one was laughing. The extent of the drought mirrored the spiritual desolation of the nation, but everyone thought it was the prophet's fault, not their own. How

hard it is for us to acknowledge our own backslidings! And how easy it is to blame those whom the Lord has risen up to bring a message of repentance!

After three and a half years of drought and desolation, Elijah called for a final showdown with the religious order of the day at the top of Mount Carmel: Set up a sacrifice on the top of Mount Carmel, put no fire under it, and call upon your god to send down the fire to consume the bullock. The god that answers by fire would be declared as God.

Elijah was alone. All the other prophets of God had been killed, with the exception of a secret remnant who were in hiding, so it was 850 of the priests and prophets of Baal against a solitary prophet of God (1Kings 18:19).

Israel, at the time, was a small, rural country, so such a large amount of priests of Baal meant that these had to have been the local church leaders from every small town in Israel. These were the men who performed the marriage ceremonies for their daughters and sons, baptized the children, and led their local churches. They knew them by name. They were the leaders of the communities. But they had all acquiesced to the false religion of the day. They had no idea they were not right with God. They actually thought Baal would hear them and send down fire to show this caustic, judgmental old prophet of Jehovah that they were the ones who were truly right with God.

Where are the courageous Elijahs of today? We are so accustomed to the religious systems that rule our localities that anyone who stands up to declare them as apostate is rejected as fanatical, judgmental, and extreme. As with Elijah, the message of the fear of God is often considered divisive among many in the modern church, while a compromising message of love without righteousness is considered kind and godly. We have chosen laxity while the prophets of God have to run for their lives.

Elijah knew that the time had come for God to show His righteousness.

The priests of Baal went first. Dancing around their altar, they called upon Baal to send down fire, but nothing happened. All day long they cried, even cutting themselves to get Baal's attention with their blood, but there was no answer from Baal. Nothing happened.

After the failure of Baal's priests, Elijah rebuilt the altar of God. The altar of God had to be built with natural stones, not cut by human hands, because the true altar of God could not be built upon man's religion but upon a foundation built by God.

He then called for four barrels of water.

Remember now, this was in the depth of a devastating drought. It had not rained for three and a half years. The rivers were dried up, the crops were dead, and animals were dying. In addition to that, this sacrifice was taking place on top of a mountain! Where were they going to get the water for Elijah? Well, they would have to go all the way down the mountain to the sea to get it and then haul it back up to the top of Mount Carmel.

Elijah then poured the water that was brought onto the sacrifice and then called for four more barrels of water. And then for another four barrels. Twelve barrels of water were to be poured out on the altar! Wherever they got water, the effort must have been extremely difficult.

What was God saying? Water, as I mentioned, is symbolic of the Word of God. Is it hard for you to get your daily reading of the Word of God? No matter how difficult, it is an absolute necessity, because the fire of God will not fall on your sacrifice until it is drenched with the water of the Word of God.

There will be no strength, no depth, no wisdom, and no faith to sustain a real move of God without it. Relying on programs and other plans to bring about a move of God is like those priests of Baal. I'm sure they meant well. I'm sure they thought they were the ones who were right with God. But they did not offer a true sacrifice, according to the truth of the Word of God, and that made them idolaters. Only when we approach the service of the Lord according to His Word will He allow us to succeed so that God and not man will get the glory.

7
Step 4 The Call to Battle

IN THE OLD Testament, two silver trumpets were used to call the assembly together:

> If ye go to war in your land against the enemy that oppresseth you, then ye shall blow an alarm with the trumpets; and ye shall be remembered before the LORD your God, and ye shall be saved from your enemies. (Numbers 10:9)

> Blow ye the trumpet in Zion, and sound an alarm in my holy mountain: let all the inhabitants of the land tremble: for the day of the LORD cometh, for it is nigh at hand. (Joel 2:1)

The trumpets were used to call the people together for various purposes: solemn religious services, new commandments or announcements, and beginnings of feasts or festivals. When they were used to blow an alarm, however, it was to gather the people of God to go to battle. When God calls out to us in the book of Joel to sound an alarm in His holy mountain, He is calling us to war.

The weapons God gives to Christians are mighty through God to cast down everything that exalts itself against the knowledge of God. Paul described our sword as the Word of God, our breastplate as our righteousness, our helmet as our salvation, and our shield as our faith (Ephesians 6:10–14). We are called out as warriors to fight the good fight of faith. The conflict of light against darkness is a central theme from Genesis to Revelation and defines our calling as soldiers of the Lord of hosts. This is war, and we will not be discharged from it until we die.

We cannot be true warriors if we do not have something to fight for. Our heart will not be in it, our resolve will not be complete, and our courage and determination will fail unless we are willing to risk everything for the kingdom's sake. That will not come to a church that has not gone through the steps of recognition, desire, and repentance. Only once we have travailed through those phases will we be ready to fight to the death for the truth of God.

The call from God goes out:

> Blow the trumpet in Zion, sanctify a fast, call a solemn assembly: Gather the people, sanctify the congregation, assemble the elders, gather the children, and those that suck the breasts: let the bridegroom go forth of his chamber, and the bride out of her closet. Let the priests, the ministers of the Lord, weep between the porch and the altar, and let them say, Spare thy people, O Lord, and give not thine heritage to reproach, that the heathen should rule over them: wherefore should they say among the people, Where is their God? Then will the Lord be jealous for his land, and pity his people. Yea, the Lord will answer and say unto his people, Behold, I will send you corn, and wine, and oil, and ye shall be satisfied therewith: and I will no more make you a reproach among the heathen. (Joel 2:15–19)

This is a call for serious prayer. This is not prayer for a sore foot, a new job, or more money. This is a call to storm the throne of God for a revival for the entire land. Gone are the superficial considerations of this world and the satisfactions with "church as usual." This is a call for war.

The people in the army that Joel described (Joel 2:2–13) are outrageous, rude, brash, uncompromising, and nothing like what we see in our pews today. They care nothing for what the world offers, and they are not worried about who is offended by their fierce message of repentance. Their fire is lit from the altar of God and will not go out until He returns. Nothing will stand in their way. The Lord has commissioned them and utters His voice before them. They will usher in the coming of the Lord with the strength and power of His zeal.

Does this kind of intensity sound like what we hear from the pulpits or on television today? This is not the kinder, gentler gospel that our pastors feed us with. This is the zeal that consumes us and whips the moneychangers from the temple. It will not easily reside in our complacent churches, for it will find no common ground there. It is a fire that is designed to burn the chaff and purify the land.

This kind of ferocious warfare is generated by the same kind of prayer. Easy quiet times of prayer will not burn hot enough to ignite this fire. Having a little talk with Jesus will not break through the doors of the throne room to forge an army like this. This takes the strong, contending prayer of warriors who will agonize with tears and crying out to shake the foundations of heaven for a move of God. This is the kind of faith that declares, "I will not be moved; I will not be denied; I will not give in. I will grasp hold of the horns of the altar and claim the promises of God until heaven moves and the earth shakes and God pours out revival!"

Before we take arms to rush to the streets in full battle gear, we must understand that the battle will not be won on the streets until it is won in the prayer room first. And it is not just prayer, but prayer that contends until it receives the answer. Power in God comes from a hard-won victory in the prayer room, and without that power, all we will show to the lost is a carnal self-righteousness devoid of the Spirit of God. If we want a move of God, then we need to move God. The flesh profits nothing. The most eloquent orator in the world may convince the mind, but only the Spirit of God can touch the heart.

You can have the best fishing pole and the best bait in the world, but if the fish aren't hungry, they won't take the bait. Prayer is needed to move the Spirit of God to stir up a hunger in their hearts for truth before we will find souls ready for salvation. If we attempt to run out in our zeal before we have secured the victory in the prayer room, we will accomplish little.

Those old-fashioned prayer warriors used to talk about how they would "pray it through"—all the way through—until they got an answer from God. Somewhere in our modern ways of doing things, we have lost that ability to crash through the gates of heaven. We say we have faith, but faith is not just believing that God can do anything. Any fool can believe that. True faith is believing that God *will* move and refusing to stop praying until He does! Anything less than that is not faith but presumption.

But do we see that kind of faith today? Gone are the all-night prayer meetings that continued all night long until the dawn broke through for souls to be saved. The desperation of Rachel's cry has become a whimper. And until we come to that place of total commitment with no compromise, we will not have the drive to take us all the way through to the victory.

We have allowed our complacency to dilute our zeal for souls, and as a result have castrated the manhood of the church. We no longer pray like the warriors we were called to be. God has called us as soldiers, and we should pray with the intensity of warriors to break down every demonic resistance, to break through every spiritual barrier, and fight for this revival we are so desperate to see established. The Lord said:

> Turn ye even to me with all your heart, and with fasting, and with weeping, and with mourning: And rend your heart, and not your garments, and turn unto the Lord your God: for he is gracious and merciful, slow to anger, and of great kindness, and repenteth him of the evil. Who knoweth if he will return and repent, and leave a blessing behind him; even a meat offering and a drink offering unto the Lord your God? (Joel 2:12–14)

Joel called for a complete sanctification of the church and a total commitment to serious prayer. This can only come from those who are desperate for a move of God. They can be satisfied with nothing less than revival for the entire land. This is the point that God has brought them to. It is not flipped on like a light switch but is refined through the fire of an entire process that has burned out all other cares and desires. Nothing else matters. Like Rachel's cry we must say, "Give me souls lest I die!"

> Blow the trumpet in Zion, sanctify a fast, call a solemn assembly: Gather the people, sanctify the congregation, assemble the elders, gather the children, and those that suck the breasts: let the bridegroom go forth of his chamber, and the bride out of her closet. Let the priests, the ministers of the Lord, weep between the porch and the altar, and let them say, Spare thy people, O Lord, and give not thine heritage to reproach, that the heathen should rule over them: wherefore should they say among the people, Where is their God? Then will the Lord be jealous for his land, and pity his people. (Joel 2:15–18)

It is at this point that God hears our cry and answers. For the children of Israel in Egypt, it took over four hundred years to get to that place of desperation before they would cry out to God. But when they did,

God heard their prayers and sent the deliverer. How long will it take today's church to get that same place of desperation? Will God have to send a wicked pharaoh to kill our children to bring us to our knees?

But when we do, He will hear.

8
The Greatest Revival of All Time

THE PROMISE OF God is this: if we will seek His face in true repentance, He will hear us and answer us and show us great and mighty things we know not (Jer. 33:3). God wants revival much more than we do.

> Yea, the Lord will answer and say unto his people, Behold, I will send you corn, and wine, and oil, and ye shall be satisfied therewith. . . . Fear not, O land; be glad and rejoice: for the Lord will do great things. Be not afraid, ye beasts of the field: for the pastures of the wilderness do spring, for the tree beareth her fruit, the fig tree and the vine do yield their strength. (Joel 2:19, 21–22)

In Joel 1, God cut off the corn (the Word of God), the wine (the Spirit of prayer), and the oil (the anointing of the Holy Ghost) from the church as a judgment, because the church had let the harvest of souls perish. Judgments are designed not only as a punishment for sin but also as a call to righteousness. But He promises to restore the corn, the wine, and the oil that has been withheld from the house of God if we repent and call out to Him for mercy and restoration.

Our separation from God has kept us from discovering the secret, hidden treasures in the Word (the corn) that only the Spirit can reveal. Imagine the riches we have wasted because we have not walked deeply in communion with Him! But now imagine the excitement of experiencing a river of wisdom that will be revealed as we dive into the Word of God. Faith comes by hearing, and hearing by the Word of God, but because our ears have been stopped up by our worldliness, our faith has been diminished. Now, however, our ears will hear and our faith will reach new levels that will unleash the supernatural in our lives and in the lives of those we touch.

The wine of God is that deep communion in prayer with Him. We have read of how our forefathers would agonize in prayer with tears for hours, even all night with God. These men were not able to pray like that simply because they had strong willpower or exercised strong discipline. That takes an anointing and a power from God that they had to seek. The Spirit of God gave them the drive and desire to push past the limits of mind and flesh to contend in prayer to that degree. That drive has mostly disappeared from the church today, but God says He will send it again.

The thrill of breaking through to the throne room of God after strong, contending prayer is like nothing you can ever experience by just having a "little talk with Jesus." It gives you a victory and a joy that energizes your walk with God. You now walk with the tread of a conqueror to break down all the walls of the enemy. Your confidence in answered prayer knows no limits, and even mountains are cast into the sea because you now have faith in God. That is because you have been there in His presence and the frailty of this world's reality is now ripped away. You can stop the sun, stop the rain, call down fire, and call down the latter rain of revival.

The anointing oil of the Holy Spirit that Joel said God will restore has been absent for so long we don't even know what we are missing. As a result, we are satisfied with dry preaching, didactic teaching, and a structured church with no life. We have convinced ourselves that the answer is in theological scholasticism and that educated degrees will suffice instead. Twentieth-century author and revivalist Leonard Ravenhill said that we once had preachers with no degrees but plenty of heat, but now we have preachers with plenty of degrees but no heat.

The anointing that has been missing will again begin to flow and life will reenter the church. Imagine being so excited over the message that you can't wait to get back to services, so much so that you now have to have church every day. Sundays will not be enough. You will be telling everyone you meet about how exciting it is! Hungry souls will finally come to get saved, not because of our doctrine or faith, but because they can see the fire in our eyes. The prophet Isaiah said that the spirit would "be poured upon us from on high" (Isaiah 32:15). This is it; this is the outpouring from on high that Isaiah spoke about. This is revival.

The fig tree and the vine will once again yield their strength, and as the sap flows through us, we will bear much fruit and will no longer be as a barren woman. The rain that will fall will bring forth life out of the desert. But not just the rain, for He will send the former rain *and* the latter rain together:

> Be glad then, ye children of Zion, and rejoice in the Lord your God: for he hath given you the former rain moderately, and he will cause to come down for you the rain, the former rain, and the latter rain in the first month. (Joel 2:23)

Joel 2:23 is a key verse that foretells a great revival coming in the last days. After Joel's call for the church to repent, he then calls to them to rejoice. Once the church has repented and cried out to God in desperate sincerity, the way is opened for the Holy Spirit to pour out upon her. Now God can "pour out the Spirit from on high" as He promises in Isaiah 32:15.

Joel says that God has already given us the "former rain". What is that "former rain"? That was Pentecost! But God is going to send not just the former rain as in the Day of Pentecost, but He is going to send both the former rain *and* the latter rain together. Brother, it ain't just gonna rain; it's gonna pour! A second day of Pentecost is coming to the church that will be far greater than the first one.

After the fire fell down on the sacrifice on top of Mount Carmel, Elijah told Ahab, "There is a sound of abundance of rain" (1 Kings 18:41). That sound is the sound of the mingled prayers of the saints ascending up to heaven, crying out for God to save souls. When you hear that sound, the rain is not far behind. This coming revival will be fueled by an unprecedented desperation for God to forgive us, restore us, and to win the souls we have neglected. It will be a powerful sound. And the answer will be an outpouring of rain as never seen before that will usher in this last great revival.

Along with the rain, Joel said that "the floors shall be full of wheat" (Joel 2:24).

Which floors will be full of wheat? The threshing floors of our churches! Souls are the harvest, as Jesus pointed out to His disciples. We've already discussed how the harvest must be brought into the threshing floor where it is processed to separate the wheat from the chaff. The job of the church is to produce a pure kernel without the chaff. These floors won't be half full or mostly full; they will be packed full of souls coming in to ask Jesus Christ to be their personal Savior. The altars will be full, the pews will be packed, and once again, there will be standing room only as people rush to God, dying to get saved.

And the vats shall overflow with wine and oil (Joel 2:24).

Not just a lot, but overflow! The Spirit of God will overwhelm our capacity to lose ourselves in praise. Very few today know what it is like to have the Spirit of God flow over you so much that you lose yourself in it. You can't stand up, you can't think, you can't speak anything but resounding praises to God. You become literally drunk on the Spirit. Even the very air will shimmer from the glory of God.

Stretch your imaginations as far as you can, but the things God will do will still be astounding in our eyes. He will do things we have never seen or imagined. This revival will be supernaturally incredible ... and wondrous:

> Ye shall eat in plenty, and be satisfied, and praise the name of the Lord your God, that hath dealt wondrously with you. (Joel 2:26)

He will restore the years that have been lost. He will raise up the valley of dry bones (Ezekiel 37). He will restore His precious bride and call her to Himself again in the greatest love story of all time.

9
Practical Steps

HERE ARE SOME practical steps to get you started in the right direction:

1. Read the Bible Every Day
The first practical step to help condition the church and believers is disciplining yourself to read the Bible. The most important tool God has given us is His Word. Reading the Word of God is where the drive for revival begins. This is where we get our power. Without it, we don't even have the power to pray, never mind know what we are praying about.

God will deal with you through His Word about the very things you will face that day. Your day will go much smoother and easier when you start your day in the Word. When you don't, you will notice that, not only does everything seem frustrating and more difficult, but so much time seems to be wasted.

Here are a couple of practical steps for jump-starting your reading.
Read a chapter of Proverbs every day. Start your reading each day with a chapter of Proverbs. There are thirty-one days in most months and thirty-one chapters in Proverbs. Read the chapter that corresponds to the day's date. Proverbs will give you wisdom and will speak to you when you find yourself in difficult situations.

The Lord says that those who seek Him early shall find Him (Proverbs 8:17). Discipline yourself to do this the first thing in the morning. Once this habit has taken hold, you will feel the difference in yourself.

More importantly, once the Bible has been opened, it is much easier to simply ask the Lord what else He wants you to read, and keep on reading. The hard part was finished when you sat down and opened up to Proverbs. It is so much easier to keep on reading after you have already begun. This is how you begin to build a fire inside your heart.

Form Bible-reading groups. You can really have fun with this while at the same time strengthening each other and the whole church. There are two ways to do this.

Have a night set aside at the church for the pastor or someone in leadership to hold a Bible study. Better yet, have one every night. This is discipleship in its purest form. You should have a leader who knows the Word of God and has a certain measure of authority so the meeting does not get squandered as a talk session or as a venue for unlearned members to spout off their stuff and get tied up in vain jangling or debate.

Another effective practice is to form small groups to meet in each other's homes for dinner and Bible reading. Everyone brings something for the meal. What an opportunity for fellowship! You get to break bread with your brothers and sisters, have a good meal, and sit around the table and take turns reading a chapter of Bible. You will soon be looking forward to having this party every week. You will deepen your understanding in the Word, strengthen the bonds of fellowship within the church, find support from your brothers and sisters, and have a wonderful venue to invite others to join you. Unsaved souls can also come for the meal and end up getting saved, and young Christians will find themselves absorbed in a brand-new loving family. This works on so many levels!

2. Assign a Daily Prayer Hour

The old saying is true, "If you don't pray, you won't stay." Without a disciplined prayer hour that you have assigned to yourself, you will always be distracted or tied up doing something else. The devil will never give you time to go pray!

Nearly every powerful man and woman of God throughout time got up early to seek the God's face. So get up early and pray! Proverbs tells us, "...those that seek me early shall find me" (Proverbs 8:17)If you wait until a more convenient time, you will end up without prayer and without that time with God.

Set aside a specific time. Make yourself get up and start praying during that hour. If you have trouble, then find a brother or sister who will covenant with you to get up and meet at the church or some other private place to pray together every day. You might even find that there are several others who also need the corporate discipline to meet together. You might start a prayer group that begins to break down old walls of flesh and laziness that had always hampered your prayers before. Then watch the powers of heaven begin to move for you in ways you never expected. This is the call that God is crying out for in Joel 2. Prayer is essential for any revival to ever take place.

Once the powerful momentum of prayer begins to roll, start looking for an opportunity to link up with believers in other churches in your community to establish a twenty-four hour/seven-day-a-week prayer chain. This will bind the churches together in your community and will present a united front to beat down the powers of darkness. What a powerful testimony this is! It will not only strengthen your entire community but will also douse Satan's attempts to create division in the body of Christ. The prophet Joel said the army of Christians in the last days would not thrust one another and would not break their ranks (Joel 2:8). In other words, there would be a cohesive unity throughout the body and that we must foster unity. Prayer is an exceptional tool to bring us into spiritual unity.

There is something powerful about a 24/7 prayer chain that moves God. He must love the constant scent of that incense from the prayers of His children. Whatever it is, I can testify that it does move Him, and it will start the wheels of revival turning.

During the Jesus Movement in 1969, we established just such a prayer chain in the little hippie church I was part of in Hollywood, California. Everyone had a prayer hour assigned to them that they were responsible for. We prayed around the clock for over ten years for God to send in souls to get saved. And He sent them. Over the course of that initial ten years, we saw over one hundred thousand souls come to the altar and give their hearts to Jesus. I have always believed that our never-ceasing prayer room was the furnace that fueled that revival that ultimately went around the world and won untold multitudes of souls during the seventies.

3. Foot Washings and Holy Communion
There is something incredibly powerful about a congregation that is bound together in the Spirit. The first Day of Pentecost came when the brethren were all in one accord (Acts 2). I believe that the second Day of Pentecost will come when the church is once again bound together the same way. One of the best ways to find that unity is by having an old-fashioned foot-washing. Jesus Himself set the example and commanded us to wash one another's feet (John 13:1–14).

The Bible teaches us that whenever we have a problem with another brother or sister, we should go to that person and humble ourselves and make peace with them. It does not matter who was originally at fault or who was right or wrong. The sin of spiritual pride knows no such distinction. This is how Satan causes strife and division in the church and, in doing so, destroys any hope for revival.

Go to that person you have a difference with, ask them to forgive you if you have done or said anything wrong that offended them, and ask to wash their feet. This will break your spirit of pride like nothing else can. Once you have done that, any and all differences or offenses will completely dissolve and a bond will be established between you that will destroy whatever Satan has tried to create.

Now imagine doing this church-wide. Pick a time, gather the whole church together, break out the wash basins and towels, and wash each other's feet. You will experience a cleansing through the whole church and a freedom in your spirits that will allow your faith to soar. It will free the Spirit of God to flow.

Holy Communion has a similar function. Remember, Scripture tell us that we are to have communion not only with the blood but also with the body, your brothers and sisters in Christ. Before you take communion, take a time out for everyone to have a chance to go to anyone they have a problem with and ask forgiveness. Again, it is important to remember that it is not about who is right or wrong; the goal is to heal the wounds in the body and seal up the divisions that the accuser of the saints has tried to create. Paul warned us that taking communion with sin on our souls causes us to be weak and sick (1 Corinthians 11:30). Hatred and variance with our brother or sister is a grave sin in God's eyes because He said we would be known by the love we have toward one another.

How many times are we admonished to love our brothers in the Gospels and in 1 John? We are also told that our love for God is contingent upon our love for our brother or sister (1 John 4:20). This is a big deal with God, and if you want to see God move in your church, you must clear away any cobwebs of bitterness and reestablish your love for one another.

4. Assign Overseers over New Christians
The pastor of any church cannot and should not be expected to do everything in the assembly. There must be overseers in the house of God to watch over the church, seasoned men and women who have the spiritual discernment to perceive right from wrong. Too much is at stake to allow anything to slip through unnoticed and unresolved. That includes maintenance of the church, taking care of the needs of individuals, and watching for encroaching weaknesses that can slip in among the flock, especially in the young and the weak. Make sure leaders are appointed to help keep the church healthy.

Jesus said that His desire is that we would bear much fruit and that our fruit would last (John 15:16). What good would it be to win souls and then let them fall by the wayside because no one in the church cared enough about them to take care of them? We should be as committed to tending to the young in the Lord as we would be if they were our own children. Part of the instruction in the Great Commission is to teach new converts everything He has taught us (Matthew 28:19).

All newly saved souls should have a mature Christian assigned to them to help show them how to serve the Lord. He or she should be like an older friend, committed to read with them, pray with them, take them out witnessing, and watch over them. It doesn't have to be a deacon or elder to do this but anyone who has been actively saved long enough to know and understand the basics of how to serve the Lord. One of the greatest blessings I've experienced as an older Christian is watching young Christians grow in God.

If we don't take care of our young, why would we expect God to send any more of His precious souls to us? This is the heartbeat of revival: the winning *and* the raising of new souls.

5. How to Invite People to Church

Revival is not about feeling good, having wonderful services, or even about miracles. It is about winning souls. To do that, we have to share the gospel with them. It's not an option or something you can ignore. It is central to the whole concept of the gospel.

When I am preaching at a revival conference, I usually spend an entire service on this one thing alone. Using passage after passage to prove, according to the Word of God, if you do not have mercy on the lost, then you may find yourself facing the Mercy Seat of Christ without enough mercy to pass over it. If you want revival, this is what revival is about: Give me souls, lest I die!

Do not make the mistake of making witnessing something difficult to do. You do not have to worry about being a preacher, knowing a volume of scriptures, having the answers to a bunch of oblique questions, or even having to convince anyone to get saved. All you have to do is invite them to come to church. That's it! Just invite them in. Simple and easy. Jesus instructed His disciples that when you have a feast invite the lost, the sick, and the maimed (Luke 14:13). Just tell them to come and let them meet Jesus.

It must be understood, you have to have a fire burning in the church before you start bringing in new souls; otherwise the souls that come in are likely to walk right back out. They want the real thing, not some cheap imitation. Once the fire is burning, however, it is easy to win souls, because you are already excited about what is happening at your church! They don't listen to the words being preached or read the gospel tracts you hand them nearly as much as they see Christ in you. When you are excited, they can see it in your eyes. It is your spirit that speaks to them more than anything else.

You don't have to rely on fancy, expensive gospel tracts. The church I was involved in during the seventies won a hundred thousand souls in ten years, and all we had was rubber-stamped, ragged paper squares we handed out on the streets. You don't have money? Neither did we. You're probably better off without all the fancy religious stuff anyway.

You can do this. Just get a rubber stamp with your church's address, service times, and phone number. Stamp up a bunch of invitations and just head out to the street. If you can afford a box of business cards with your invitation on them, even better. All you have to do is hand them out and keep going. If someone stops you to ask a question, then great! If not, you just keep on going. Those little invitations will take on a life of their own, and God will use them to deal with and convict the souls He has put before you. All you have to do is invite them. God will do all the rest of the work, if you let Him.

Open-air crusades, where crowds are drawn into an open area with music so they can then hear the gospel preached, work a lot better in Africa than they do in America. Times have changed, and so do methods. If open air crusades work for you, then by all means, hold them. If they don't, do something else that does work. Try walking down the street handing out cards or tracts that invite them to your services. That doesn't work for you? Then ask God. This is His campaign not yours, so ask Him to direct you.

Don't be surprised at what the Lord will lead you to do. And don't let the devil tell you what you can and cannot do. I have stood outside the FBI building in Washington, DC, to hand out tracts. I couldn't go in, so we prayed for them to come out to us. Guess what happened? It was the time of the Super Bowl victory parade for the Washington Redskins, and they let all the employees out to see the parade. All of a sudden, hundreds of FBI employees came pouring out of the building, all headed our way! And there we were, handing them the gospel.

It doesn't really matter how you reach them. Whatever you do, however you do it, by all means, witness. Your life and theirs depend on it.

6. Have a Vision
The Bible says that where there is no vision, the people perish (Proverbs 29:18). You have to have a vision to know where you are going that will help you overcome the obstacles that will be thrown in your path. A vision is more than just a revelation from God or a goal to attain to. A vision has substance that is birthed out of desire. It drives you past your flesh, past your fears, and past your unbelief. A vision creates victory.

You must be able to not only see past your horizons but to grasp the reality of it with a faith that produces a passion in you that will dare to believe God enough to say *yes!* to the impossible. Your vision has to be greater than yourself, greater than your Sunday church attendance, and greater than your religious image. Your vision has to be about a revival to energize the church and win the lost to Christ. Anything less than that is simply playing church.

Jesus told us to deny ourselves, pick up our cross, and follow Him (Matthew 16:24). His vision was the cross and the victory that was won for the souls of all mankind. How can we follow Him if we have no vision set before us to strive for? We need a vision or we will perish in our own mediocrity.

Our lives are often limited by the horizon we can see around us. If you want a real Holy Ghost revival, you must set your vision beyond the horizon you can see with your eyes and look with your faith. Act like you believe the Bible. Have the courage to believe God, and take Him at His word. Only then can a path be set that leads to victory.

The Lord commands us to "write the vision, and make it plain upon tables, that he may run that readeth it" (Habakkuk 2:2) Write it down! Until it is put on paper, it doesn't really exist. And then post it where it can testify to your face throughout the day. Now you know where you are going and why. Now you have a compass to guide you in the direction that will help you fulfill your calling in God.

The same is true for the church. Your church should have a vision that defines the ultimate goal you want to achieve. Post it on the wall of the church so everyone can see. Now your church has a goal, has a direction, and has a passion that is set before you so that you know what you are doing and why.

The price for revival is high, and without a vision, you will not have the passion to pay that price.

7. Are You Born Again?

This book would not be complete without a call to salvation. You may be an on-fire Christian and saved for many years, or you may have just picked up this book from curiosity but have never given your heart to the Lord. It may be that you have sat in church all your life, but you've never made that final commitment to ask Jesus to save your soul.

Whatever the case may be, if you are not born again, the Bible is clear that you will not enter the kingdom of heaven. There is no way around it. Jesus said that if you try to get to heaven any other way, you would be like a thief and a robber (John 10:1).

Paul outlined the prayer for salvation for us:

> If thou shalt confess with thy mouth the Lord Jesus, and shalt believe in thine heart that God hath raised him from the dead, thou shalt be saved. For with the heart man believeth unto righteousness; and with the mouth confession is made unto salvation. (Romans 10:9–10)

Let me be completely clear. Just saying a bunch of words will not save you. Rather than a form prayer that someone else wrote, it is simply the cry of your heart through your lips, crying out to God that He will hear you.

The elements of salvation are simple:

Repent of your sins. All of them, sincerely, and be ready to forsake them forever. Jesus paid the price for your sins, and you must understand that the price He paid for you was not cheap and easy. Don't let your sorrow for sin be cheap and easy either. You must be broken for your sins. If you think you can say a prayer and like magic be instantly converted, you will find that empty words bring empty results. You must come to the foot of the cross in a brokenhearted state, crying out for God's mercy. Only then will He hear you.

If you are not at that brokenhearted state and not ready to turn from your sin, then pray for God to send you Holy Ghost conviction to bring you to that place where you are ready to give it all up and cast yourself down at the foot of His cross. Believe me, He will answer you.

Confess Jesus Christ as your Lord and Savior. Acknowledge that He alone can save you, and that God raised Jesus from the dead by the power of the Holy Ghost.

Ask Jesus to save you and wash you in His Blood. It is His blood that is the atonement (payment) for sin, and it is His blood that broke the back of the power of sin in your life. There are no works you can bring to the altar that will pay the price for your sin—only the blood of Jesus.

Believe. Belief constitutes more than just a superficial acknowledgment. It is a total commitment to this truth that you have discovered. God hears the cry of your heart and is more ready than you will ever know to save your soul. He can hear you, and He promises in His Word that He will answer you. He will save you.

Thank God. In our praises and thanks, faith is released and the doors to heaven open up. Raise your hands and praise God for your salvation.

The prayer below is meant only as an example for you. If you say this prayer or whatever heartfelt prayer you choose, make sure you say it from the bottom of your heart. You are not looking for a repetitious adherence to a tradition but to a supernatural conversion to Life. Pray:

> *My Lord and my God, have mercy upon my soul, a sinner.*
>
> *I believe Jesus Christ is the Son of the living God and that He died on the cross and shed His blood for the forgiveness of my sins.*
>
> *I believe Jesus rose again from the dead by the power of the Holy Ghost and sits on the right hand of God.*
>
> *Come into my heart, Lord Jesus, and wash all my sins away with Your blood. I invite you into my heart as my personal Savior and will follow you the rest of my life.*
>
> *Your Word says You'll turn no one away, and that includes me. Therefore, I know You've heard me, and I know You've answered me, and I know I'm saved.*
>
> *Thank You, Jesus, for saving my soul.*
>
> *Amen.*

Now raise your hands and thank and praise the Lord for saving your soul. Open your heart and receive the life-giving Spirit of God.

Now that you have asked Jesus to come into your heart, you need to find other born-again Christians to fellowship with who will also help you to grow in the Lord and help you seek for the Baptism of the Holy Spirit.

Pray for God to show you a church to attend. Do not separate yourself from the flock. God has a place of safety for you. Ask Him where He wants you to attend church, and He will lead you there.

Conclusion

THE THINGS I have related to you in this book are all written in the Word of God, and they shall come to pass. There have been great revivals in times past, but the great revival that is promised in Joel 2:23 and Isaiah 32 has yet to be fulfilled. Six times the prophet Joel identified the time for this revival would be just before "the day of the Lord."

This timing makes perfect sense, because the spiritual conditions just before the time of His second coming will be the same as they were just before His first coming. The prophet Isaiah said that Jesus was a root out of dry ground (Isaiah 53:2). A spiritual drought left all of Israel dying of thirst for a new move from God just before Jesus' first coming. There were synagogues and Pharisees in every town, but just the rumor of this prophet rising out of Israel caused thousands of simple farmers to drop their plows and walk long distances to the Jordan River to hear Him speak. It will be even drier just before He returns, the perfect setting for revival. I don't know how long it will last or when it will break forth, but I do know it is coming.

But it is not coming to the church world as we know it today. God will give the churches a certain space of time to repent, and they will not repent. Why should they? They do not feel they have to. Revival would be nice, but they don't feel the desperate need to have one at any cost. The sad thing about apostasy is, the same blankets of comfort and ease that the church covers herself with are the same blankets that cover her ability to see. She is the last to realize how dead she is, even though it is blatantly clear to everyone around her.

The church of Laodicea, as Jesus described in Revelation, is alive in our churches today. She thinks she is rich and increased with the blessings of God, but she is blinded by her comfort and cannot see how far she has fallen from where she once was. Denominations that were once forged in the fires of revival have now become social organizations—sophisticated, rich, organized, theologically correct, and proud of a heritage they no longer possess. Their pride will not allow them to repent, and so the flames on their candlesticks slowly fade away as they sit complacently in the increasing shadows that grow around them. The fire that once burned so hot has simmered down to coals and ashes that are now only lukewarm (Revelation 3:16).

God will raise up stones in their place. Spread across the land is a Gideon generation that wants something more than just "church as usual." These are the people God will call out of those dead institutions to forge Joel's army for this last great battle between God and Satan for the souls of man.

There is no question that this last great revival will come. It will come. The Holy Spirit is sounding the trumpet. The question is, will you answer the call? If you do not, then you will end up standing on the sidelines watching as the fire of God falls on some other church that was willing to do what you were not. The choice is yours.

Friend, we are living in the most exciting time of all history. A terrible spiritual war is coming, and it is for such a time as this that we are called to stand in this final battle. This is the final culmination of the conflict that has gone on since the beginning of time. Heroes will be forged during this final battle that will shine throughout eternity. I pray that you will be one of them.

Answer the call, rise to the challenge, and have the courage to believe God for the greatest revival of all time.

About the Author

Dalen Garris got saved in 1970 at the beginning of the Jesus Movement. He has been involved in ministry across America since then. He has been bringing the message of revival across Africa since 2003, but he has now begun to turn his attention back home to America to bring those same revival services that made such an explosion in Africa. He is willing to take this message anywhere people are hungry for a God-given, Holy Ghost revival.

Dalen has settled in Waxahachie, Texas, with his wife and three grown daughters and their children. You can contact him and find his pamphlets, books, videos, and podcasts at www.RevivalFire.org.

Dalen Garris
Revivalfire Ministries, Waxahachie, Texas
www.RevivalFire.org
dale@revivalfire.org

www.ingramcontent.com/pod-product-compliance
Lightning Source LLC
Chambersburg PA
CBHW070632300426
44113CB00010B/1743